THE SAVVY BRIDE'S GUIDE

OTHER TITLES BY ALICIA YOUNG

Two Eggs, Two Kids:
An Egg Donor's Account of Friendship, Infertility and Secrets

(PARASOL PRESS LLC, 2015)

The Savvy Bride's Guide: Your Wedding Checklist

(PARASOL PRESS LLC, 2014)

The Savvy Girl's Guide to Grace:
Small Touches with Big Impact—at Home, Work and in Love

(PARASOL PRESS LLC, 2013)

the
SAVVY BRIDE'S GUIDE

Simple Ways to a Stylish & Graceful Wedding

ALICIA YOUNG

PARASOL PRESS LLC, TEXAS

Young, Alicia.
The savvy bride's guide. Simple ways to a
stylish and graceful wedding / by Alicia Young.
—2nd edition.
p. cm.
Includes bibliographical references and index.
LCCN 2015902426
ISBN 978-0-9855950-5-0 (pbk.)
ISBN 978-0-9855950-4-3 (ebook)

1. Weddings—Planning—Handbooks, manuals, etc.
2. Brides—Handbooks, manuals, etc. I. Title.
II. Title: Simple ways to a stylish and graceful wedding.

HQ745.Y68 2015 395.2'2
QBI15-600061

PARASOL PRESS LLC
PO Box 980456, Houston, TX 77098-0456
Book design by Monroe Street Studios
Cover art © Anne Keenan Higgins
Author photo by Elizabeth Shrier. © 2014 Alicia Young.

Printed in the United States of America
First printing 2014; second edition 2015
10 9 8 7 6 5 4 3 2 1

For Holly, a stunning and gracious bride.

Once upon a time, a starry-eyed maiden awoke and declared, "It's time to find my prince!"

She searched near and far, but each suitor fell short. Finally, she went to a sage, renowned throughout the land for his wise words.

"Make a list," he told her, "and include all the qualities you seek in your betrothed."

So the maiden sat under a tree and the words flowed: kind, generous, hard-working. This was easy!

Then she returned to the sage with her list.

She was surprised when he didn't motion to read it.

"Be sure to become those things," he counseled, "and you will attract the same."

CONTENTS

INTRODUCTION

❦

GETTING MARRIED IS A UNIVERSAL RITUAL—yet how, when, and where we pledge "I do" is a wickedly fun, deliciously personal choice. While a wedding is a joyous occasion, it also takes planning to navigate many decisions in an often compressed time. This book will guide you through myriad options, from the moment you're engaged to the time you comb the confetti from your hair. Whether it's tips on choosing your bridal party or the key elements to look for when you "scout your location," you'll find it here.

Even before pledging your vows, the way you are proposed to—or the way you pop the question yourself—is rich with possibility. Have you always dreamed of a classic down-on-bended-knee proposal? Does your heart race at the thought of your loved one asking you on a stadium jumbotron screen before forty thousand people? How about during a hot-air balloon ride or atop the gorgeous hill you hiked on your first date, with a carpet of wildflowers at your feet?

My husband, Jon, proposed in the middle of a job interview we both attended. Really. We had been living together when he was offered a position as a live-in housemaster assistant at a boarding school. We met with the principal, who told me, "I'd love to have you here too, but you can't live in sin. I'll give you a month to get married." I began to retort, "I think *not* . . ." (with my best arched eyebrow), when next to me I heard, "Sure, we'll see you in a month." I swung around to see Jon smiling and shrugging, "Why not?" So we had two weddings. First came a small legal ceremony on a cliff top overlooking the ocean. This idea might sound lovely—it *was*—but we forgot about the wind factor:

my hair billowed above me in a cylinder, and I vaguely resembled Marge from *The Simpsons.*

Later, we had a traditional church service. And somewhere between the two, we enjoyed a honeymoon safari on a shoestring. As you can see, I'm open to doing things out of order if it works.

Oh—a little confession up front: I almost derailed a crucial part of our church ceremony. Vows tend to be rather straightforward, but mine took an unexpected turn. When the time came, I gazed lovingly into Jon's eyes and declared, "I, Alicia, take you, Father Patrick. . . ." Jon was stunned, but laughed and graciously overlooked it. The priest was speechless, though he later said it was the best offer he'd had. I would hope so! How many brides end up proposing to the clergy?

THE SAVVY BRIDE

You might wonder: what differentiates a Savvy Bride from all others? In short, a graceful approach to this special day. She delights in a good celebration as much as the next girl, but knows this wedding is just the beginning of her and her spouse's lives together, not the destination itself. And she gently understands that curious paradox of weddings: that they're both unique and commonplace. When this bride-to-be weds her beloved, it's special because it's *their* day, but because many of us marry, she doesn't behave as though she's the first or only woman ever to go through it. This lends a healthy perspective to both cherishing the delights and accepting the challenges (familial, budgetary, faith based, or otherwise) that might lie ahead.

A Savvy Bride is also aware of MY-itis. You know, as in it's MY day. MY dream wedding. MY dress (okay, we'll give you that last one). She refers to OUR wedding. OUR day. OUR honeymoon, at least some of the time (written with a smile).

SIDESTEPPING COMPETITION

Are you planning a wedding around the same time as a friend, relative, or colleague? Keep in mind how a little fun comparing notes can lead to competition. You'll want the relationship to last long after your respective celebrations, so resist rivalry, however subtle. Be happy for the other couple and toast their choices.

When it comes to receiving advice from friends and relatives, listen respectfully and sort the wheat from the chaff. Stay open to what they're saying, then discard what doesn't work for you. Keep some pleasant, noncommittal stock phrases up your sleeve.

YOUR BRIDE BRAND

Relax. I'm not using the word "brand" here to suggest you view your wedding as a cold business decision. But whether you know it or not, we each have a brand that broadcasts to others how we see ourselves. Imagine sitting at your favorite outdoor café and enjoying people-watching as you sip. You probably can sum up in one or two words the feeling you get about people as they saunter, stride, or bustle past. Edgy? In command? Creative?

Now turn the focus on yourself. Consider your walk, your speech, your general dress in everyday life, and the message that they broadcast to the world about who you are.

Many women find the type of bride they want to be is a natural extension of that essence, while others want to adopt a more dramatic departure. Some of the most easygoing girls want to feel like Queen for a Day or a princess. I once worked with a mousy administrative assistant who dressed in quiet neutrals and never initiated conversation. She shocked everyone by strutting down the aisle as a 1930s vamp, with a striking diamanté headpiece and her thick, sensible spectacles replaced by lashings of dramatic liquid eyeliner.

A WORD ON GROOMS

When planning her wedding, the Savvy Bride may ponder the issue of how much to involve her groom. Many men today take an active interest and want to help with the planning and organizing of their nuptials. They might design rings, pen the vows, or contribute compelling ideas on music and menus.

But I say with affection, those with a Y chromosome have generally less stamina for wedding-related details than we do. I teased Jon, "Be at the church at three o'clock. I'll be the one in white." Sure, he was involved in the planning, but my advice would be to avoid saddling your groom with too many details if he's a little resistant. He likely won't care if the dinner napkins match the bridesmaids' dresses. It might be more his thing to organize the cars and the honeymoon, which are traditionally male duties anyway. And if your partner is also a bride, bear in mind she might be equally nonplussed.

So, with an open mind, let's get started on your wonderful journey!

PART I

Sharing the News

Chapter One

YOU'RE ENGAGED!

❧

Congratulations!

THE TRUTH IS, I'D LOVE TO pin you down right now and demand to know all the details of how you came to be engaged and what type of wedding you have in mind. I've been known to stop strangers in the street to inquire as to how they met their loved one and who asked whom and how. Well, almost.

Did you have any clue that a proposal was brewing? Did you leave hints, or did he? Did you find a little velvet box stashed away, à la Movie of the Week, and graciously feign surprise when the moment arrived? Or did he go for maximum drama and punch? Maybe you saw the viral video of the man who made a complete "movie trailer" about meeting his love and then screened it at a local theater where his unsuspecting sweetheart had gone to watch the latest blockbuster. Or perhaps you heard about the doctor who organized an elaborate fake photo shoot for his model girlfriend, only to gate-crash it and get down on bended knee? Not to be outdone, a different model got the surprise of her life. She glided down the runway in bridal couture, only to find her boyfriend waiting at the end of it, ready to propose. Creative, for sure, but the sweetest and most romantic proposal can be simple and secluded.

Was yours a private occasion, or were you asked in front of family, or a packed restaurant, or through the glass of a prison visit? (Only joking.)

We've all seen the good, the bad, and the truly shocking of wedding proposals, but a Savvy Bride-to-Be takes it in stride and sees the touching intent behind any sweetly endearing fumbles. Hopefully, you weren't the lady who discovered that her engagement ring was hidden in her dessert . . . after she swallowed it.

What's important is that the question was genially asked and graciously accepted. You're engaged! You're floating and can't stop gazing at your left hand. Enjoy! It's a magical time, and you both deserve this happiness.

MAKING THE ANNOUNCEMENT

You want to shout it from the rooftops: we're getting married! So what's the best way for you to spread the word? Again, the details of your announcement can be as individual as you like, but there are a few key people who would appreciate hearing it in person, if possible. Both sets of parents, of course, and your grandparents too would love a visit and the opportunity to take delight in your news before others hear about it. I appreciate you know this already, but the best intentions can fly out the window when your head is swimming with visions of bling, bridesmaids, and bouquets.

Global Glimpses

In **Spain**, it is customary for the groom to present the bride's father with a watch after his proposal has been accepted. In sharp contrast, many **Chinese** communities discourage any sort of timepiece as a gift; it is felt to be deeply insulting, as the hands are said to tick toward the person's death.

Grooms in many **South American** countries bestow on their brides a gift of thirteen gold coins (*las arras*), also known as unity coins.

Next, tell your best friends—if not in person, then at least by video chat if they're across the country or overseas.

We can't ignore the popularity of social media to trumpet announcements big and small, but hold off just a moment. A Savvy Bride takes the time to tell close friends and loved ones personally. It's such lovely, exciting news, they'll be touched to share it with you right then and there, not logging on later to see your email/post/tweet between folding laundry and making dinner. A longtime friend shouldn't have to find out about this major life event by noticing that you've changed your relationship status on your social media profile.

Kate and I have been friends since we were twelve. I didn't expect to be in the bridal party—she has four sisters—but I was hurt when she didn't call or even email the news. I learned about it when she posted a picture of her sparkler. —BRENDA, FORT WORTH, TEXAS

⟶ Global Glimpses

In days past, **Welsh** wedding tradition dictated that a besotted young man take much care to carve a "love spoon" from a single piece of wood. It would feature intricate designs such as Celtic knots, keys, or bells. He would then present it to his intended, and if she accepted it, they were engaged. Love spoons remain popular today in wood but also in other materials such as pewter.

MEETING THE PARENTS

Hopefully, your parents have had a chance already to meet your partner, and vice versa. But that may not be the case if you met your fiancé in college out of state or while you were posted out of town for work. Much is made of meeting the parents, and while it is significant, it needn't be stressful or overly formal. Short of planning a trip, a simple video chat would be a low-key way to make introductions. This is also a great opportunity to organize a relaxed brunch, afternoon tea, or dinner at home, so that each side can get to know you as a couple.

THE RING:
COUNTERING MYTHS AND INDISCRETIONS

We were never actually engaged, but I still breezily shared with Jon some new research: a study showed the bigger the diamond, the stronger the marriage. He didn't buy it (literally or figuratively), but he still teases me. Lots of girls dream about a rock the size of an ice cube, but, honestly, a Savvy Bride is more interested in investing in her marriage than the ring that symbolizes it. You'll be every bit as delighted with a slightly more modest adornment that doesn't require its own bodyguard. Or wheelbarrow.

And beware the tricks of the advertising world: In the mid-twentieth century, an international diamond merchant famously launched a marketing campaign promoting the idea that an engagement ring should cost the groom a month's salary. Over the years, that one month became two months, and now it's three. You won't want your intended to have to sell a kidney on eBay to afford your sparkler.

A Savvy Bride-to-Be will anticipate the most common reactions to her ring and have a few stock phrases at the ready to deflect less-than-stellar comments. "How many carats?" or some variation on that theme seems to top the list of perhaps well intended but inappropriate questions about a new engagement ring.

I was so excited to head into work the Monday after Marc proposed. But I was stunned when a new colleague—I'd known her all of two weeks— wasted no time inquiring, "What's it worth?" "It's worth the world to me," I replied, without missing a beat. I surprised myself, but the cheek of her to ask in the first place! —SKYLAR, CHELSEA, LONDON

Marion T. of Brisbane, Australia, said she was stunned to be asked, "Is it real?" She found silence quickly dealt with that. Other less-than-stellar responses include "Mine's bigger" and "Why? Are you pregnant?"

If your proposal did indeed come at a particularly intimate time, be prepared to gloss over that when sharing the news of your engagement. You and your partner could always agree to a general version of events to share with others. We're in an age when many people make the most private of moments as public as possible, but a Savvy Bride resists peer pressure.

Tirza K. shares that Jewish couples traditionally have very simple wedding bands, unadorned by engraving or precious gems. The symbolism of the ring lies in its unbroken unity. Its modesty also means couples are less likely to forgo a ring due to an exorbitant cost.

Perhaps your partner presented you with a ring his grandmother wore, or perhaps it was some other family heirloom. If you love it—wonderful! If not, the situation calls for a little diplomacy. You might have it reset in a more modern design, or pair it with other stones. Even if you can't see a way to salvage it, don't dash his hopes then and there. Enjoy the proposal! You'll know when to broach the subject privately, ideally before others are shown the ring.

If you go shopping together, do a little research first as to color, carat, clarity, and cost. Check that your retailer is a member of a respected professional association and has the relevant license to deal in precious metals and stones. Your local Better Business Bureau or other consumer agency can usually provide a check as to any disciplinary action.

A LONG OR SHORT ENGAGEMENT?
The best length for engagements will probably always be a polarizing issue, and the way a couple arrives at their decision—and how they define "long" or "short" in the first place—will be as personal as their own story. Let's review some of the main advantages on either side.

The Case for a Long Engagement (Twelve Months or More)
If you feel like circumstances are nudging you toward a longer engagement than you would otherwise choose, spare a thought for Scandinavian couples. This region is known for engagements of three years or more, reflecting a thorough and deeply considered approach to marriage.

Many couples like the idea of having longer to save for their big day, and that's understandable. Also, considering how many decisions need to be made, giving yourself more time eases the pace and the pressure. But here's a more pressing reason for a long engagement: simply to get to know your partner on a different level. Unless you're Elizabeth Taylor, you'll likely only ever be engaged once, so why rush through this phase? This especially holds true for couples who have known each other less than a year before deciding to marry. A longer engagement allows your relationship to deepen, as you have the opportunity to see each other under different circumstances (the loss of a loved one, a promotion awarded or declined, and other instances when life throws a curve ball).

More practical elements can benefit from, or require, a longer engagement. Perhaps family or friends will need to travel from overseas; they'll probably need more notice to accrue vacation and make travel plans. The venue you have your hearts set on might be booked for a year or more; or your wedding might coincide with a relocation for work or for one partner to join another.

The Case for a Short Engagement (Twelve Months or Fewer)
Others see no need for a long time between the engagement and the I Do's: the decision has been made, so let's do it! They tend to see the compressed time frame as less likelihood of getting overwhelmed. As long as you have a general idea of the wedding's key elements (when, where, and how), this can work. After all, we can create an entire human being in nine months, so it stands to figure that a celebration can be planned in the same time or less.

Our wedding was not at all standard. Everything was done at the last minute (dress, rings, etc.), and as a result, it was perfect. We were all happy and enjoyed the moment, which is something I wish more people would do. It was small and delightful; everyone there played a critical part—from driving to photography to ironing a shirt. —DANIELA, RIJEKA, CROATIA

PREMARITAL COUNSELING
Imagine for a moment that you're shopping for your dream home. You wouldn't sign up for such a big investment without doing your homework, would you? You'd want to know that the house has a good foundation, that it will meet both your needs and those of any children that might come along, and will endure through the years. You would look

for evidence of small cracks that could prove to be a sign of larger problems looming. A marriage raises many similar issues.

Investing in a few counseling sessions, either faith based or secular, can help you both navigate this next chapter in your life. You might be surprised about what you didn't know about each other, whether you have been together less than a year or more than a decade.

A good counselor, rabbi, or pastor can help you anticipate some of the milestones and questions to come. Do you hold similar values around family, money, and education? Maybe you were raised in a particular religion, and while not actively practicing, you'd like to expose your child to some of its elements. Have you decided whether you'll take your partner's name, keep your own, or hyphenate? Is it a big deal, or no deal at all? Does either of your families have a history of serious illness or children with special needs, and you're curious about exploring genetic counseling? Is your partner supportive of you continuing your career after children? Does one or both of your professions involve a lot of travel, which may force one parent to carry more of the daily load? How do you resolve disagreements?

In our own premarital counseling session, Jon couldn't recall his family's religion. Methodist? Church of England? Salvation Army? Exasperated, the priest simply made us promise that our children would be raised Catholic. (Who knew we'd forget to have them?)

When it comes to premarital sex, I belong to the try-before-you-buy brigade. That said, I sincerely applaud those who choose to wait until their wedding night to get intimate. It's so rare, and very special. If that's a decision you have reached together, let no one dissuade you.

Chapter Two

CHOOSING YOUR BRIDAL PARTY

❦

MANY OF US ALREADY KNOW who we'll want standing beside us when we take our vows. Maybe you've known her since middle school, when you made a pinkie pledge. But unless she's absolutely sure, a Savvy Bride resists the urge to ask someone to be maid of honor or a bridesmaid at that same moment she shares the good news. On further reflection, she might find that her college roommate, while a dear friend, is not someone she's as close to these days. Ask yourself why you are considering this person: if a sense of obligation plays a role ("We've drifted, but after all, I was *her* maid of honor. . . ."), you might prefer to find a different way to include her in your day. It needn't be tit for tat: the flow of life can take us in different directions, and a Savvy Bride can gracefully find a way to acknowledge their shared history on the day or in the preparations. A reading? A special toast? Anything but asking her to look after the guest book; as lovely a gesture as it is, few people relish the idea of waving a pen about, hoping to entice a scribble of good wishes as guests waft by.

THE BRIDESMAID TRADITION

You may have heard about the origins of wedding attendants as clones. In days gone by, it was considered both good luck and a safe bet to have attendants looking almost identical. Some believed if the ravishing bride stood out too much, a passing demon might snatch her as his own.

Ladies in Greece have their own twist: rather than having single girls as bridesmaids, a matron of honor and her children would accompany the bride to the service. This was not only a show of loving support, but a symbol of fertility for the happy couple's future.

Meanwhile, in the United Kingdom, blushing brides are often surrounded by very young attendants, from tweens down to preschoolers.

~⊘ Global Glimpses

In keeping with the general **UK** tradition, royal weddings tend to feature attendants quite a bit younger than the bride—and the trend seems to be moving to younger still.

When England's Queen Elizabeth II pledged her troth in 1947, her bridal party boasted eight bridesmaids, most of them far junior to the twenty-one-year-old royal. A generation on, Lady Diana Spencer (later Princess Diana) had five bridesmaids, a sprinkling of young girls and teenagers. More recently, Kate Middleton (now Catherine, Duchess of Cambridge) was famously attended by her sister, Pippa, and a pair of adorable three-year-olds.

OTHER BRIDESMAID CONSIDERATIONS

What about a pregnant bridesmaid? Not to worry! If the friend seems to have changed her mind in the interim, a Savvy Bride asks gently if she is still comfortable being part of the bridal party. Heavily pregnant in a summer wedding? It will likely make for a tired and uncomfortable attendant. If she wants to continue, welcome that and proceed gracefully. She didn't get pregnant to throw off your wedding pictures.

In keeping with that theme of thoughtfulness, resist suggesting a thinly veiled fitness kick if your bridesmaids are pleasantly plump. Perhaps also sidestep any temptation to present them with some sort of bridesmaids' handbook. It might seem a little too presumptuous or too pointed to be presented with a book-length manual of duties. You'll want your maid of honor and bridesmaids wonderfully enthusiastic, not stressed out.

Bridesmaids' responsibilities needn't be overwhelming. They act as a general sounding board for ideas and help choose the dresses. They might host or help plan a shower, and also the bachelorette party. The maid/matron of honor will sign the wedding certificate as a witness. Your attendants also help by chatting with guests or fussing a little over elderly relatives who might enjoy a little company while others are dancing.

Going Pro

If you need extra help, from a virtual chat to someone standing by your side, check out bridesmaidforhire.com. "Professional bridesmaid" Jen Glantz came up with the novel way to offer her services and share her extensive wedding experience with time-pressed brides—and bridesmaids.

THE BRIDAL SHOWER

Bridal showers are a delightful tradition to celebrate the lady of the hour. As with other aspects of a wedding, showers seems to have grown in scale and variety, but they needn't be overly elaborate or complicated. Your guests might find themselves deluged with different invitations to celebrations held by your work colleagues, college crowd, and extended family. Guests should be invited to just one shower—and only local guests at that.

I've noticed a trend to ask attendees to address their own thank-you card while at the shower. A Savvy Bride is delighted to make this effort herself.

Kirby O'Connell (styleknockout.blogspot.com) is a San Francisco blogger who has quickly carved out her place in the competitive fashion landscape. She adopted a fresh approach to a bridal shower, hosting a fun and stylish wine tasting to toast her sister Mallory and her pending nuptials. The family hails from the San Francisco Bay Area, but the celebrations were kicking off in New York City. O'Connell arranged for a selection of California wines to be shipped to the Empire State. She researched and delivered a short presentation on each grape, with everyone invited to jot notes. They then enjoyed a blind tasting, with the ladies matching tastes and labels based on their notes from the presentation.

Prizes were awarded to the two that guessed all of them correctly. Sounds like a delicious and relaxing way to get everyone involved. And having a designated driver allows guests to enjoy a drink without worry.

THE BEST MAN AND GROOMSMEN

In centuries past, a potential groom would enlist a close friend to help him kidnap his bride; this man would then stand beside him at the ceremony, ready to draw his sword and shield in the event the bride's family or other tribal members showed up in protest. Today, the swords have been laid to rest, but the supportive role remains. Like a maid or matron of honor, a best man contributes ideas and lends a supportive ear.

This close friend (or brother) traditionally takes the lead on planning the bachelor party and enlists the help of the groomsmen. He safeguards the groom against any trouble or behavior he might later regret. On the day itself, the best man ensures the groom gets to the church on time. He guards the wedding rings and carries the checks to honor any outstanding balances for the emcee, officiant, or the band. The best man also toasts the maid or matron of honor and the bridesmaids.

AVOID LANDING YOUR BRIDAL PARTY IN DEBT

An overarching tip for good planning: keep expenses for your bridal party front of mind when making decisions that affect them. The honor of being your attendant shouldn't—and needn't—leave a close friend or relative in debt, or working extra shifts to cover the expenses.

Being a bridesmaid is a time-honored tradition—and used to be a relatively economical one. Friends would gather for lunch, or at a bar, or perhaps at someone's home to fête the bride-to-be. Today, we see multiple showers, destination bachelorette trips that stretch over days, and enough expenses to make you cry into your wedding cake. No one needs to spend the GDP of a small nation to enjoy a fabulous and memorable event.

Bridesmaids traditionally pay for their dresses, but a Savvy Couple plans to cover whatever they can of the bridal party expenses.

There are plenty of ways to trim costs while sacrificing none of the style. You could select a color and invite your bridesmaids to choose their own dress and style in that hue. This is a kind way to go, especially when different budgets and body shapes come into play. Shoes needn't be satin covered and dyed to match the dresses—it can look either fabulous or a little matchy-matchy. Instead, black pumps will do credit to all, and they're probably already sitting in everyone's closet, waiting to dance the night away.

You might consider paying for the girls' hair and makeup. In a similar vein, instead of giving the groomsmen a hip flask (so cool, but likely destined for the back of a drawer), you might gift them the rental of their tux, or pitch in half.

One of my bridesmaids complained nonstop about the color and style of dress. We paid for the material, her hair, and makeup, and suggested black shoes. She still moaned about the small amount to have the dress made! And she was always too busy to get fitted—she finally went to the dressmaker three days before the wedding, and got it back less than twenty-four hours before she wore it down the aisle. If my brother-in-law hadn't needed a partner, I would have waved her goodbye. —STELLA, BONN, GERMANY

PART II

Key Considerations

Chapter Three

MONEY MATTERS:
THE BUDGET

❦

UNLESS YOU'RE A ROCKEFELLER or a royal, you'll need a wedding budget, and the sooner it's clarified, the better. And a little grace in raising the subject of a budget will save hurt feelings and family drama.

Our weddings are often our first major financial outlay, except for perhaps a car or college expenses. It's only natural to get caught up initially in the romance of it all, but a Savvy Bride tries to take a pragmatic approach to a budget. There will be plenty of opportunity for creativity and whimsy!

HAVING THE CONVERSATION

The discussion about finances usually comes in two waves: first with your partner, then with your parents.

Be aware that planning a wedding brings myriad financial choices and decisions in rapid fire—and that can spark long-buried or unacknowledged attitudes and habits about money in your family or as a couple. We all have a relationship to money, whether we approach it generally from a point of abundance or scarcity. Is one of you a saver and the other a splurger? Are credit cards for emergencies or for everyday purchases? And let's define "emergency": are we talking a last-minute dress for Saturday night, or dental work you can no longer postpone? The ways in which you deal with your day-to-day budget, both good and bad, are likely to be magnified when you're planning your nuptials. The manner in which you and your partner resolve these conflicts (Shout 'n pout? Frank discussion? Silent treatment until one caves?) will be a sign of things to come, so start as you mean to continue. And not to be terribly unromantic about it all, but a wedding is very often followed by a mortgage application, so a Savvy Couple strives to keep their credit scores pristine.

Then, there's the talk with your folks. If you're very lucky, you won't even need to broach the subject of money, as parents will most often want to contribute and will happily mention their intent and scope early on. Personally, I think bridal couples today should pay for as much as they can, especially if they haven't had to foot the bill for college. Whatever the approach, a Savvy Bride keeps a few things in mind.

How close are her parents to retirement? Or are they retired already? Even if they're financially comfortable, they might have already received their last big paycheck. Be kind and mindful of that. Anyone living on a fixed income could find it challenging to find the resources to contribute to a wedding. The same goes for a person supporting a dependent, such as an aging mother or father.

If their contribution is decidedly more modest than what you were hoping for, resist any urge to wail, "But you paid for everything for Sophie's wedding!" Maybe your sister got the whole nine yards covered, but today your parents find themselves navigating decidedly different financial straits. They will do the best they can, and a Savvy Bride gracefully accepts that with thanks.

In days gone by, the bride's family largely footed the bill. Thankfully, that's not assumed to be the case today. For starters, many couples already live together before marriage and have their own jobs, dual incomes, and a fully stocked home.

Whoever Pays Gets a Say

There's also the issue of "contribution equals control." Usually, if someone pitches in significantly toward the wedding, they'll expect some influence over key elements, whether the guest list, the venue, or even the overall theme. Weigh this carefully and decide together what you're willing to concede for financial support.

～ *Finances:* QUICK TIPS

♦ Open a dedicated wedding savings account; make automatic contributions to it by establishing direct debits from your salaries over the next year or set number of months. This system makes it easier to track deposits and will help ensure that you keep up with regular bills amid the wedding costs. You can't plan your special day in the dark when you've had your power cut off!

♦ Aim to start your married life as close to debt-free as possible, at least in relation to wedding costs. You won't want to be still paying off your wedding reception when your second child arrives. Student loans can be demanding enough.

♦ Prioritize and maintain perspective. Agree on the top three nonnegotiable elements of your wedding, and it will be easier to separate the priorities from the puff.

♦ Build in a 10 percent buffer to your budget for unforeseen expenses.

♦ Remember meals for the DJ, photographer, and others who will provide a service on the day.

ASKING FRIENDS TO DONATE THEIR TALENTS

Your friend is a talented, intuitive photographer, and you want her to weave her magic on your special day. You're comfortable working with her, and it would help you to save a bundle on a professional service. It seems so easy and convenient a decision. That said, think twice before asking friends or relatives to make a gift of their talents, whether they lie in photography, hairstyling, baking, music, or something else. A Savvy Bride considers how many times this friend may have been asked—or outright *expected*—to perform this service. Might it be more graceful to allow this friend the gift of witnessing your day without lugging around heavy lenses or a lighting kit? The same goes for pals who are hairdressers or makeup artists, always corralled into the same role.

Even if you're both enthusiastic about it, consider this: The upside is that you get a gorgeous gift and feel your friend is intimately involved in your day. But if you're dissatisfied with any aspect of your friend's contribution, addressing it can be especially awkward, as the stakes are simply higher. You wouldn't believe the number of friendships that wobble or disintegrate altogether because the photos or videos are never forthcoming or take far too long. It's one thing to chase down a vendor; it's another if that vendor is your cousin.

WHEN CHIC MEETS CHARITY

Ismini and Mark Svennson took an inspiring approach to their wedding. Instead of a lavish celebration, they opted for a simpler affair—and redirected their budget to perform kind acts in each of the fifty US states. In turn, they established a charity, StayUnited, in part to honor Ismini's father, who believed passionately about helping others and who sadly suffered a fatal heart attack while at a charity event. Learn more about their quest at stayunited.org.

Another bride shares:

I wish I had skipped all the hoopla and taken the money my father offered instead. Not only would I have saved a ton of arguments with my mother, but we would have had a nice savings deposit.

I polled a few people several months after our wedding. Not one person could tell me the color of the bridesmaid dresses, the flowers used for the centerpiece, or even what we served at the reception!

—KATHY L., HOUSTON, TEXAS

Global Glimpses

In some parts of **Canada**, "socials" are held as a way to raise money for the nuptials and celebrations. Members of the bridal party fan across town, soliciting donations, rustling up sponsorship, and selling tickets. The fundraiser culminates in an evening of potluck dinners, music, and dancing.

Germans start budgeting for a wedding early. When a baby girl is born, cuttings and saplings are planted in her honor. The mature trees are then sold once her wedding date is set.

An **Indian** diamond tycoon has made headlines for several years by funding the marriages of women from backgrounds marked by abject poverty or other hardship. Recently, he financed the nuptials of more than one hundred couples in Gujarat state in western India. More typically, social workers and community leaders will organize group weddings in poor communities, to minimize the cost and dowry associated with a wedding.

Chapter Four
FAMILY DYNAMICS

M ONEY IS JUST ONE ELEMENT in a wedding. Any major celebration calls into focus a range of decisions that can bring family
dynamics to the fore. A Savvy Bride is again mindful of this. No matter
the occasion, we are who we are, and we approach milestones as an
extension of our daily selves; a homebody won't morph into the life
of the party, and a splurger won't suddenly become penny-conscious
overnight.

PARENTS

It's said that parents, well, *parent* in reaction to their own upbringing—
keeping the good, ditching the bad as they see it. If that's true, then,
by extension, your parents might view your wedding plan in light of
their own ceremony and circumstances. Maybe they had a quickie service at the courthouse, or in the maternity ward, or as one of them
was deployed—and ever since, your mother has dreamed of you getting
married in a sumptuous gala affair with full band and fine dining. She
might see your nuptials as the chance for a do-over of her own. Or perhaps your parents had a lavish soiree, only to divorce a few years later,
and so they view a big wedding as a frivolous expense. If you have no
siblings, or at least no sisters, you may face another challenge. Perhaps
you dream of a low-key elegant affair, but you're facing pressure as the
only daughter to have a showstopper reception.

Cut them some slack and try to see their words, actions, or advice through the prism of their own experience. Listen, even if you disagree; this is a huge deal for them. (Several brides have told me that they noticed a mild depression in their mothers in the weeks after the wedding!)

This might surprise you, but not receiving your parents' full financial support can be a blessing. I once interviewed a young couple whose parents had paid for every penny of their wedding. It didn't stop there. For wedding gifts, one set of parents bought the newlyweds a house; the other parents furnished it—right down to the can opener in the kitchen drawer. They then added two new cars in the driveway. I remember thinking, "What do these people have to work toward together?" It seemed like they'd never know the joy and satisfaction of working hard, making do with thrift-store items, and working up to new things they would treasure all the more. (Humor me. I feel 105 years old saying this, as if I should be swinging on a porch chair with a straw in my teeth.) They divorced within a few years, and I've always wondered how different it might have been if they were less coddled and had to work together to see their dreams come to fruition.

In any case, the day will arrive, if it hasn't already, when your folks will have to wave you goodbye, so be sensitive to how hard that can be for some parents. Others will make light of it. As one father joked, "We're not losing a daughter; we're gaining a bathroom."

SIBLINGS

A wedding can bring you closer to your siblings, as you plot and plan a wonderful day. On the other hand, it might bring up issues for a sister who, say, has been waiting for years for her partner to pop the question, or has just ended a relationship she felt was heading to the altar. You don't need to apologize for your wedding, of course, but it can make all the difference to stay sensitive to circumstances that may stir up sibling rivalry or jealousy.

Sometimes a wedding date falls in the midst of some family spat, from a small but sticky issue to something more drastic. The key here is to have someone neutral speak to the parties concerned, before the day itself. Ask the mediator to keep it light (no one likes a lecture) and to adopt an approach that already reflects trust: "We know things have been testy for a while, but we'd really appreciate your help in keeping the issue off-topic on the wedding day." Naturally, both parties will snort with derision at the thought they might be anything less than ideal guests, and let them do so. The seed has been planted, and that's what matters.

Other times, your diplomatic skills will be tested by relatives who are sure you won't mind if they bend your instructions. It might be a sister or a close cousin who is certain you didn't mean *them* when you said "no children," or the godparent or aunt who decides to bring an extra guest along.

EXES

Accommodating divorce and remarriage in the family brings its own challenges. Resolve to play neutral in the face of ultimatums such as "If he comes, I won't." It can take willpower, but decline to buy into someone else's grudge or unresolved issues with something like this: "Our wedding will be a lovely day, and we want you to be part of it. We hope you choose to come." Repeat as necessary; feel free to be a broken record on the subject. Unless legal restraining orders are in place to force the issue of someone's presence or absence, make *them* decide.

Many times, grace will simply come to the fore, and you will not need to worry, as this lady shares:

The setting for my stepson's wedding was Maui, a semi-central destination for his American family as well as his bride's, who hailed from Australia. The hotel was small but perfect. A swimming pool was out back, just steps from the beach. My four-year-old twins were set to don tuxedos as ring bearers. My daughter-in-law-to-be was so precious you could eat her with a spoon. For weeks beforehand I agonized about sharing pool time and meals with my husband's ex, but when she arrived in the lobby shortly after we did, my husband grabbed my hand and held on tight. After that, everything else fell away, and I did what I was there to do: celebrate a beautiful union.
—CYNTHIA HOUSE NOONEY, PIEDMONT, CALIFORNIA

ASSORTED BLACK SHEEP

If a "black sheep" in the family will be attending the wedding, be prepared for the possibility of anything from passive-aggressive comments to a scene worthy of a soap opera finale. Create a buffer zone, and have someone on hand who is at least broadly aware of the situation (without having to know intimate details) to act as a peacekeeper if necessary; if problems arise, they can change the subject, ask the person to dance, or suggest a drink on the terrace.

We run a family business. Trouble had been brewing with a strident cousin for a few weeks, but we didn't expect this the week before my wedding: he filed suit for unfair dismissal. I wasn't there, but there was an almighty shouting match along the lines of "How dare he?" And the wedding was days away! We reviewed the seating chart and made some tweaks to create more space between him and my father. Then we appointed someone to speak to each of them beforehand. Calm prevailed—at least, until the following Monday. —GEMMA, RALEIGH, NORTH CAROLINA

Chapter Five

WHEN, WHO, WHERE, AND HOW?

❧

LET'S LOOK MORE CLOSELY AT some of the key elements that will need your attention. Questions of when and where to tie the knot, who you would like present to share your day, and how you'd like to celebrate are varied and important decisions. Enjoy exploring your options—your wedding day is on the drawing board, and you get to be as creative as you wish in how you celebrate!

WHEN?

There are many things to consider when choosing a date: Do you have enough time to plan? Enough time to save? Allow yourself sufficient advance notice to book the venues you want for the ceremony and reception. It's a not a sprint to the church, temple, courthouse, or mosque. Give yourselves plenty of time to enjoy planning; less pressure means more fun.

What time of year do you have in mind? Would you like to be a spring bride, or have you always imagined a winter wonderland? As you would imagine, different seasons bring with them a variety of flowers and foliage, weather, and other elements.

Consider whether your potential dates coincide with a major holiday, sports event, or religious observance. It's always delightful when guests are enjoying themselves and in the moment, not craning their necks to hear the score without being caught. Also, certain times of year might be out for religious ceremonies: for example, Catholic weddings are not usually held during Lent, the somber forty days before Easter Sunday.

Timing might also incur extra charges. A wedding on Valentine's Day will likely add to your flower bill, and pledging vows on New Year's Eve can also come with a hefty price tag (on the upside, you'll forever enjoy your anniversary celebrations being followed by a holiday sleep-in.)

TIP:

When you've confirmed a date, advise your HR department at work. It might have implications for your health insurance and other factors.

What time of day would you prefer? A beachside wedding at dawn sounds delightful; just be sure to enjoy an early night, as you'll likely be up at 4:00 a.m. for hair and makeup. Mid-morning weddings are beautiful, but by noon, the sun will be directly overhead. This means there'll be lots of natural light, though you'll all have shadows under your eyes when the photos are taken. Sorry, but it's worth knowing. As a bonus, a brunch or lunch reception will be considerably less expensive than an evening affair.

How about an off-peak wedding? Consider a ceremony off-season or perhaps on a Friday night. One couple I interviewed had a midnight service in a chapel, and used over four hundred candles for lighting. They designed a gorgeous ceremony bathed in the flicker of candlelight: visually stunning and very romantic (and they did get a professional photographer who knew how to work around the lighting issues). If this sounds like you, short winter days mean you can go from an early evening ceremony straight to dinner.

Once you've selected your date and had the venues confirmed in writing, send out your save-the-date cards. Family and friends will appreciate as much advance notice as possible.

∼ Global Glimpses

Not for the faint of heart: In some **Mongolian** communities in China, couples wrap their hands around a knife to slay a chicken in unison. The appearance of the chicken's liver is said to hold clues to an auspiciously timed union. If the organ is stunted in growth, discolored, or diseased, the pair must continue the ritual until a healthy liver is revealed. On a lighter note, once a date is divined, some couples choose to commence the ceremony itself at thirty minutes past the hour, so that their future together begins as the clock's hands are swinging upward in optimism.

For **Italians**, Sunday is simply the gold standard.

The **Irish**, meanwhile, favor Leap Day (February 29) as a lucky time for a woman to propose or for a couple to take the plunge. Another auspicious marriage date in Ireland is St. Patrick's Day (March 17), the feast day of the country's patron saint. You won't need to serve a green cake, but emerald-colored beer or spirits will be welcomed!

Astrology plays an important part in the timing of milestone events for many people in Asia. In **India**, for example, families of newborns have an astrologer draw up their child's future in intricate detail. Years later, when a wedding is proposed, parents of the bride and groom again consult an astrologer to divine the best time for a union. Similarly, in **China** the astrological calendar is consulted for auspicious days on which to get married, taking into account the birth year of each partner (Year of the Horse, Pig, Monkey, etc.). A go-between oversees a lengthy engagement. Inquiries, research, and gifts are exchanged through this intermediary.

WHO?

We probably all have relatives we only ever see at events such as christenings, weddings, and funerals (a trifecta also known as "hatch, match, and dispatch"). For all we know, they could scrub the oven, check their tire pressure, or coach little league while bedecked in a three-piece suit or evening gown because we've never seen them wear anything else. You never hear from them outside these events, so you might be surprised to see that your mother has included their names on the invitation list.

Enter guest-list diplomacy. Only marginally less delicate than Middle East diplomacy, this phenomenon will call on all your reserves of grace, insight, and patient negotiation. Claudia G. recalls her mother strenuously debating the merits of inviting a dozen of her office acquaintances—not even close work friends. "But they always ask about you," protested her mom. "Tell them I'm fine," Claudia replied with a smile.

Our guest list grew like a weed garden: despite our efforts to slash away, the numbers steadily grew back. Finally, I asked my parents gently, "Do they know my middle name? If they don't, I'm not sure they need to be there."
                                                    —HARRIET, BOLTON, MANCHESTER

Another Savvy Bride looks back on her day and shares this, to round things out:

I now tell friends, if in doubt, invite those "on the fence" friends if your budget allows. None of us have a crystal ball, and we've been grateful to look back on friendships that have deepened, and felt relieved that we invited that person or couple to our day.   —FAITH, BOSTON, MASSACHUSETTS

At my wedding, one guest told me sweetly, "Holly, you look beautiful." Holly is my sister, and she *is* beautiful. But it might have been nice if the guest had checked which of the Young girls were getting married that particular day! Bless.

⌒⌒ *Global Glimpses*

In **England**, some couples still invite a different type of guest to their nuptials: a chimney sweep. Legend varies: Some say a London chimney sweep saved King George II's life over two hundred years ago, and the king then declared that all chimney sweeps bring good fortune. Others attribute a similar decree to King William the Conqueror in 1066. Either way, it's now considered good luck to see a chimney sweep on your wedding day, and many hire out their services to attend the ceremony and bestow a sooty kiss on the bride's cheek or hand.

Keep in mind that typically half of your budget goes to the reception, so that will help determine how many guests you can accommodate and whether you're looking at silver service, a backyard barbecue, or one of many options in between.

Others take a high-tech approach to the number crunching. One couple made news by turning to statistical modeling to determine how many guests to invite. Of the 139 invitations sent out, their model predicted that between 102 and 113 people would accept, with the highest probability being 106. The model proved to be accurate, for 105 people ultimately showed up, just under the total capacity of their chosen venue. For those of us who aren't as mathematically adept, simply count on 10 percent of the invitees sending their apologies!

Children: To Have or Have Not at the Wedding?
You'll need to consider what role, if any, children will play at your wedding. Your preference might be to have children only in the bridal party, or perhaps you'd like to limit the child guests to nieces and nephews on both sides. Whatever your decision, make it early and give people plenty of notice to make arrangements for child care. Other Savvy Brides include children on the guest list but provide a babysitter to keep an eye on them. This is very generous, but don't feel obliged. As Taylor K. wrote on her invitations: "Plus-one: welcome. Children: photos welcome!"

WHERE?
The "where" in the wedding equation is brimming with options for your setting and location. In general, these include deciding on a particular city or town, as well as on a civil versus religious ceremony, an indoor versus outdoor wedding, and a public versus private venue.

Perhaps you're looking to "head home" where most of your relatives are based. Or you're faced with the choice between the groom's hometown and (traditionally) the bride's. If that's the case, you may want to consider a neutral place altogether.

When planning an outdoor event, always have an alternative venue in mind for inclement weather. Compile a list of phone numbers for each guest or family representative and have a friend or relative on standby to send a group text if weather forces your plans to change. Alternately, include on the invitations a statement such as "In case of rain, please meet at this second location," and reiterate it on your website.

If your wedding will be faith based, talk to your celebrant before you book a venue for the ceremony. Some religions won't allow services to be held outside in a garden; a church setting is often nonnegotiable. They can also advise whether rice, rose petals, or confetti are permitted.

Scouting potential locations is not just for film and TV producers. Check the venue's space, the presence or absence of natural light, and the acoustics. Explore access to electrical outlets for vendors such as caterers, the photographer, or DJ—both in spacing and number. Extra points if the venue has areas in which you can touch up your makeup, cut the cake, or simply slip away to enjoy a few quiet moments alone or with your partner. And take a tip from people in the hospitality industry: you can get a quick read on any restaurant or event facility by how clean the restrooms are. If they neglect that, you can be sure they're slipping in other areas, too.

If you're getting ready at the hotel or reception venue, do a dry run to time how far it is to the location where the nuptials will take place. As Mariska. T confided:

We got married at a beautiful rustic hotel in wine country. It wasn't until the day itself that I realized how far my suite was from the gardens we were to be married in, and it seemed to take forever to arrive! The green space was elevated, and I'd forgotten about the staircase leading up to it and to the reception area. Also, I thought I'd worn in my shoes enough, but I was hobbling a bit at the end, and had to rest a moment before I started up the aisle.

—MARISKA T., SANTIAGO DE CHILE

We'll explore more tips on selecting venues in the chapters on destination weddings, the ceremony, and the reception.

HOW?

While the *when* and the *where* will be decided on fairly early, the question of *how* you'd like the day to unfold lends plenty of magic and creativity to planning your wedding. This encompasses the overall theme and the feeling you want to capture to symbolize your union.

Perhaps family tradition is a country-club soiree for three hundred. Or you're imagining an intimate gathering for a dozen, with a string quartet and a degustation (gourmet tasting) menu. Have you dreamed of exchanging vows on a mountaintop, on the beach, or underwater? I once helped prepare a wedding reception for a party of ten, and each guest had their own butler. It was dramatic indeed: each attendant in livery, standing sentinel a few feet back, ready to be beckoned. Possibly overkill, but certainly memorable!

Whatever theme, mood, or approach you choose, ensure it's applied consistently throughout your colors, décor, cake, flowers, correspondence, and music. You wouldn't plan a barn dance and then decide to use silver service in the hay-strewn dining area, unless you're courting an eclectic effect.

Black tie is truly sumptuous and oh-so-glam—but will it break the bank for your guests? As well as shelling out for a gift and possibly travel and lodging expenses, will they need to rent or buy a tuxedo or an evening dress? You'll want everyone in a celebratory mood, not worrying about meeting the mortgage payment this month.

And then there's costumed theme weddings. Perhaps you've always dreamed of channeling Maid Marion (though maybe your Robin Hood is less than thrilled at the prospect of green tights). How about a medieval theme with fair maidens and jousting? A celebration worthy of Henry VIII, complete with a banquet table groaning under the weight of steaming platters, huge turkey legs, and silver goblets? You might ask guests to hire costumes in lieu of gifts, but many will feel compelled to arrive with something in hand.

Others leave behind the theatrical aspect in favor of tradition. A wedding can be a touching expression of your heritage or values—it's all a question of balance. Is there some common ground you could find to accommodate your parents' wishes? You might find a song, reading, or hymn from their ceremony to incorporate in your own. Maria S.

found a crumpled poem tucked into her parents' Order of Service in their attic; she asked a relative to recite it at the wedding, accompanied by music. Her parents were surprised and deeply touched. Elements of the ceremony, dress, music, or food could be a nod to tradition or your heritage in some way. A little compromise goes a long way. Weaving dishes from the bride and groom's family heritages into the menu is a delicious and easy way to pay homage to two cultures coming together.

Reflecting Your Values

Familial ties are surely important, but this day celebrates two individuals uniting. Perhaps you feel passionately about a meat-free celebration; if so, honor that and find a way to soothe the carnivores with plenty of tasty treats. Maybe you're dedicated to being environmentally conscious, minimizing your carbon footprint as you choose local vendors, sourcing free-trade or recycled materials. A quick search under "eco-bride" or "green bride" will yield many handy resources.

Carolina G. and Costas T. felt strongly that they would avoid the use of blood diamonds (tied to armed conflicts and human rights abuses) in their rings. Instead, the bride chose an emerald, while her groom elected to have a ring tattooed on his finger. This also served a practical purpose, as wearing a ring posed a safety risk to his job as a welder.

⌘

Planning a wedding is a joyous, if intense, time. The intricacies of the details can cause the fun to boil over into stress. A bride can feel a little overwhelmed as she "gets into the weeds" of myriad particulars. When things begin to reach a boiling point, it can help to take a breath and keep perspective. This Savvy Bride saw her wedding in very clear focus after an unforgettable period of tumult:

We were married in New Jersey the Saturday after September 11th.

I was one of those brides who loved planning our wedding. I obsessed about every detail, from the invitations to the flowers on the reception tables to the wedding favors.

But on our wedding day, those details just seemed so unimportant. So what if the flowers didn't arrive because the bridges were closed? So many lives had been lost and hearts broken just a few days before.

I told my fiancé that I couldn't get married without my family and friends. But most of them were supposed to fly from Texas on Thursday, and their flights had been canceled. So, on Thursday morning, they piled into two vans and drove straight to New Jersey. They arrived Friday afternoon, in time for the rehearsal. On Saturday morning, before the wedding ceremony, one of our guests remarked that he saw a plane in the sky, which meant flights were allowed again.

Things were slowly starting to get back into place. Newly married, my husband and I danced the night away with our family and friends. To this day, we still receive emails and Facebook messages from guests who tell us that our wedding helped them laugh, smile, and feel hopeful at such a devastating time—something they truly needed that Saturday after September 11th.

—ROSE C.V., BERKELEY, CALIFORNIA

Chapter Six

TOOLS TO GET ORGANIZED

❦

STREAMLINE YOUR CORRESPONDENCE

ONCE YOU START ACTIVELY PLANNING your wedding, you'll be deluged with subscriptions, free and otherwise, and a river of offers and promotions will flow. Keep these materials separate from your regular mail. Streamline your correspondence by opening a fresh email account so that all wedding information is funneled to one inbox, and consider renting a post office box for six months or a year for the same reason. Once on a mailing list, always on a mailing list. It will be far easier to shut down the bridal email address one day than to unsubscribe to each and every site, blog, or catalogue. Use a binder to collate all your brochures, printouts, and samples, unless you're an eco-bride and feel strongly about staying "all digital." As I've mentioned, you may want to open a separate bank account to keep track of wedding-related deposits and expenses. You'll feel part project manager, part diplomat, part accountant.

A SPREADSHEET FOR GUESTS

Keep a list of your guests' names, addresses, mobile phone numbers (an office phone number likely won't help on the day itself), and email addresses (a last-minute group message can save confusion in the event of plans changing due to weather). Just check that your guests are comfortable with you storing their contact information:

We asked my brother-in-law to be the go-to guy for any last-minute emails to the group. He was great about consolidating them—but then he hit on the "brilliant" idea to send this same group his business promotions. It was really awkward. I was fielding calls from bewildered or irate friends and family who had no need for his services. —JOSIE, CAMBRIDGE, MASSACHUSETTS

As gifts arrive, add each guest's gift to the spreadsheet; this will make it much easier to write thank-you notes.

A SPREADSHEET FOR VENDORS

Similarly, start a spreadsheet in which you list all the names of your vendors or potential vendors. Keep track of the following details:

- their place of business and contact information

- their business license to operate (if anyone is offended by you asking for one, give them a wide berth)

- notes on any consumer ratings or reviews (such as those found online through the Better Business Bureau and other consumer agencies, or on review sites such as Yelp)

- your contractual agreements (information on where the contract is stored, deposits paid or due, remaining balance, etc.)

CORE QUESTIONS FOR ANY VENDOR

A few general points:

- Research them as best you can online and through word of mouth before you make contact.

- Keep as much in writing as possible so that everyone is on the same page and a clear chain of correspondence exists in the event of any misunderstanding or failure to deliver on the agreed service.

- Copy yourself on all emails so that email content cannot be changed (rare, but it helps to protect yourself).

- When you meet with a vendor, resist the pressure to leave a deposit or sign anything on the spot. Arm yourself with someone supportive but less starry eyed about the wedding. Go away, think about it, and then review the sample contract. Highlight any clauses you don't understand and ask for clarification in writing. Any changes should be initialed and dated by all concerned, or ideally a new contract should be printed and the previous one shredded.

♦ Ask to be put in touch with previous clients.

♦ Ask about their industry experience: they should be able to give you examples of a challenge that arose and how they dealt with it.

♦ Request that their quotes be itemized. One bride was shocked to see that a caterer charged for each individual spoon, knife, and fork, as well as "cakeage" fees to cut and serve the cake.

♦ Arrange a trial run whenever possible. For example, if you can afford to, hire a photographer to take engagement pictures first, before signing any contracts for the wedding itself.

♦ In case of sudden illness or emergency, they should have an agreement with a colleague to fill in. Who are their two or three go-to people? If you're signing with an agency, you might not be sure who they will send on any given night.

♦ Always ask for a blank sample contract to review at home.

YOUR OWN WEDDING WEBSITE
A wedding website is a great one-stop destination for guests to review directions, check your registry, or simply confirm the time of the service.

However, it's nice to retain a little mystery as to the little touches that will make your day *yours*. Whether she creates her own wedding website or posts details on Pinterest and other social media, a Savvy Bride keeps some surprises up her sleeve. One fiancée launched a wedding site eighteen months before the day—with almost every last detail plastered on there for general consumption. Everyone from her guests to her dog walker could check out the bridesmaid dresses, the flowers, the invitations, even the centerpieces. Leave something to the imagination, otherwise the event might begin to feel a little too pre-orchestrated.

WEDDING-FREE DAYS

Updates on the nuptials will understandably dominate conversation as the event approaches. Having some wedding-free days can be a wonderful safety valve, both for you as a couple and for your friends and family, who have plenty of things going on in their lives too. One lady declared Wednesdays and Saturdays as bride-free zones; she still gets kudos for that years later.

Every time I caught up with Aurelia, I expected a fresh report, like breaking news, on the latest development for the wedding. And as chief bridesmaid, I was happy to listen and offer ideas. But after a while, it was like the "big day" sucked the life out of every other thing happening in our lives—hers included. She got a promotion that she later told me as an afterthought, and I tried to tell her about a transfer I was offered—but it all got sidelined. Finally, I had to call time out. —JANA, DUBAI, UAE

My sister and I live and work on different coasts, and we have a tradition of a Sunday-morning phone call to catch up on the week. Wedding talk filled the first month or two, but I loved her even more when she declared, "No wedding stuff until I hear about what's going on for you." I was really touched. As she said, we were sisters long before the white dress came up, and we'll be sisters a long time afterward. —A.J., POUGHKEEPSIE, NEW YORK

I wish I had done this! In the first month or so after we got engaged, I was like, "Sure! Ask me anything! Any time, any detail." After that, I was obviously still interested, but a little worn down. Finally, I felt myself getting a little overwhelmed. Setting some boundaries early on would have helped. —MIA, AUCKLAND, NEW ZEALAND

Chapter Seven

DESTINATION WEDDINGS

❧❧

YOU'RE SITTING IN THE LOVELY but freezing Midwest as you plan your big day, and you can't stop thinking about reciting your vows under swaying palms. Or you're watching perpetual drizzle fall in London and suddenly you just have to pledge your I Do's in sunny Spain.

A destination wedding might be across the country or across the world. A bridal toast with fresh coconut cocktails? A luau wedding, complete with Hawaiian shirts and seashells aplenty? A Kenyan soiree overlooking the sweeping plains? What could be more glamorous or more exotic? Creative possibilities abound, but a Savvy Couple carefully weighs the potential challenges and disadvantages of a destination wedding. Let's review the fundamental ones.

PLANNING AND RESEARCH

Can you afford to visit the wedding destination beforehand to meet with vendors and check out the venue? If not (and that's completely understandable), then you'll need to feel comfortable choosing the key players without meeting them first. Are emails and a few Skype conversations enough to feel confident about sending your deposits to a foreign bank account? Note also that if you have any grievances with international vendors, it might be expensive or near impossible to follow up. It might help to choose a resort or hotel chain with a location in your home city, or at least in your own country.

Risks Posed by Different Water and Cuisine

Could your destination wedding be beset by "Bali Belly," "Montezuma's Revenge," or other side effects of ingesting foreign water or food? No bride should have to deal with stomach issues on her special day (aside from a few butterflies), and the same goes for everyone else.

Weather

For tropical weddings, are you flirting too close to hurricane season? Check whether government travel warnings are issued routinely at that time of year. Ask your travel insurance agency about coverage for emergency evacuation in the event of hurricanes, monsoons, or other natural occurrences. Also consider the possibility that an extreme weather event could wreak havoc on your tropical destination even before you arrive.

Local Events and Customs

Are local elections due to be held anywhere around the date you have in mind? This can trigger political and social instability. You won't want your vows drowned out by protests or anti-Western sentiment. And this risk is not limited to foreign locales. Take it from a journalist: do not plan your New York City wedding during UN General Assembly week. You and your guests will be caught in major traffic jams and layers of extra security as foreign dignitaries come and go.

Note also that public displays of affection may not be tolerated in foreign locales such as Dubai and Singapore. In some countries, a slight lack of modesty in dress can invite frowns, even legal ramifications. A simple kiss in public may land you in hot water.

THE COST TO YOUR GUESTS

A Savvy Bride, naturally, is a considerate bride. She looks realistically at the true expense of a destination wedding to the guests. If they will need to travel by air, do they have enough advance notice to get a good deal on flights? Will it be peak season for hotel accommodations and airfares? Do they have sufficient time to request vacation days? They might also need time to apply for or renew a passport and perhaps to organize inoculations. Some hotels and resorts offer wedding packages with discounted rates, and sometimes even a few complimentary rooms. It might be a lovely gesture to offer those to your parents or to the guests traveling farthest, who presumably have the highest airfares.

Opinions differ as to which travel expenses should be covered for members of the bridal party. Some say that the bridal couple or their parents should pay for rooms for the bridesmaids and groomsmen, the rehearsal dinner, the reception (certainly), and brunch the next day. Often they also include a group activity, such as an island tour or a visit to a cultural center. Guests pay for their flights and room tabs. Others declare the hotel room is the responsibility of the guests, and I tend to agree, unless we're talking about parents, grandparents, or the bridal party.

Whatever you decide, be graceful but clear as to what is covered and what is not, so the getaway is not marred by misunderstandings. For example:

> *7:00 p.m. Friday:* Tom's parents invite you to be their guests at the rehearsal dinner on the hotel's mezzanine level.

> *Saturday morning:* Please find vouchers for breakfast enclosed. You'll discover many lovely options for lunch in the hotel and in town, just a ten-minute walk away.

> *4:00 p.m. Saturday:* See you at the wedding service! Reception to follow.

> *11:00 a.m. Sunday:* Rani's parents invite you to be their guest at brunch.

> *Checkout:* We have arranged a late departure of 2:00 p.m. for all our guests.

Even with finances addressed and costs minimized, some people still might not be able to make it. A grandparent might need a travel companion or could be declined travel insurance on the basis of age or pre-existing health conditions. For close families, this could pose a dilemma that might take a destination wedding off the table. But if these challenges can be overcome, enjoy!

Chapter Eight

INVITATIONS

❧

UNLESS YOU FEEL STRONGLY ABOUT conserving paper, I'd encourage you to bypass e-vites. A printed invitation conveys a sense of occasion and needn't be expensive. It also prevents the potentially awkward moment when the invitation is forwarded to someone else "because I just assumed they'd be invited too."

As long as it hits the note you want, be it casual or formal, an invitation can do its job with occasion and dignity for pennies. Many online samples can be downloaded and tailored, or you can make your own. Choose a good quality paper stock or try a local printer or a stationery specialist.

Weight and distance can make a difference to postage costs: you won't want to be the bride who painstakingly addressed and stamped 150 invitations, only to have them returned for insufficient postage. Even putting aside the extra expense, imagine the writer's cramp in addressing those invitations all over again in her beautiful cursive!

If you're concerned about expense, postcard stamps are typically 30 percent cheaper than a regular stamp for domestic use. One side could feature a lovely photo of you both or a wedding image, and the other could list the key information, leaving space for the recipient's name and address. Take a sample to the post office first to check the cost per region: locally, nationally, and overseas.

You might also consider using the services of a local graphic design school. Contact their administrative office or student services department, and ask them to post an ad on their site or in their newsletter. It's a good idea for your agreement to state that you own copyright to whatever they produce for you, but allow them portfolio rights.

Global Glimpses

Invitations to **Jewish** weddings are usually two sided, with one side written in Hebrew and the other in English.

In **Sri Lankan** villages, it is customary for the parents to invite friends and relatives to a wedding by presenting them with a betel leaf (*Piper betel*) in the palms of their hands. The tip of the betel leaf points to the person invited to the celebration; in contrast, if the stem faces the person, it signifies their presence is requested at a family funeral.

PART III

What Sort of Bride Will You Be?

(YES! YOU DESERVE A SECTION ALL YOUR OWN.)

Chapter Nine

DRESS, HAIR, AND MAKEUP

❧

THE DRESS

YOU MIGHT HAVE HEARD THAT a white wedding dress has long been associated with purity; so much so, that it was thought that nonvirginal brides could not or should not wear it without inviting scandal or smirks. If that ship has sailed for you, take heart: this religious meaning was actually bestowed only in the last century or so. The white wedding gown as we know it today was popularized by Queen Victoria in 1840, though there are accounts of royals marrying in white in the 1400s. White clothing has a long association with affluence, as once upon a time, only landed nobility could afford such an extravagance; workers in the field wore rough, earth-colored fabrics. Bleaching fabric into snowy hues was expensive and simply not an option for the working class to have or maintain.

Some believe that in distant times, the white wedding gown symbolized the moon, and the gold wedding ring represented the sun. Therefore, the wedding was a symbolic union of the sun and the moon.

In any case, you've probably thought about your wedding since playing with dolls, staging pretend ceremonies in grade school, or sketching a heartthrob's last name as your married name on your textbooks. What type of bride would you like to be? Old Hollywood glamour? Edgy? A barefoot maiden with a flowing white dress and sprig of fresh flowers in her hair? A fairy-tale princess, complete with meringue dress? An earth goddess?

And now, you get to shop for a wedding dress! Alas, you've probably noticed that adding the word "wedding" to anything can cause the price to treble. A lovely lace might be one price per yard, but as Christina S. observed, make that "French lace" and the asking price soars. Nonetheless, stunning and affordable options abound.

⟞ Global Glimpses

Guests at a **Chinese** wedding today are treated to three wedding gowns. The bride debuts in a traditional *cheongsam*, a slim-fitting sheath with delicate embroidery. It is most often red, as the color is considered auspicious. Afterward, she slips into a white dress in the Western tradition. She wraps up the evening in a cocktail dress, as she and the groom bid their guests goodnight.

A **Norwegian** bride traditionally wears a white or silver wedding gown. She often completes the look with a silver-and-gold crown, adorned with delicate spoon-shaped charms that tinkle as she moves. Legend holds that this gentle clinking protects her from evil spirits.

Enjoy Shopping!

Make an appointment at two or three of your favorite bridal stores so you can enjoy the staff's attention and won't be rushed. Before heading out, take time to do your hair and light makeup. You'll probably go in with an idea of what you'd like and enjoy playing with that look. But at the same time, a Savvy Bride stays open to trying on a few other styles the staff might suggest—they have a lot of experience with different body shapes and bone structures. You might just be pleasantly surprised at what feels "you."

Karen Willis Holmes (karenwillisholmes.com) is a wedding style maven whose influence on the industry resonates from Sydney to New York and London. She recommends that brides avoid being overwhelmed by taking two people along for shopping. This set the tones for fun, not frustration. Bigger numbers can be a recipe for confusion as different opinions weigh in. Willis Holmes adds: just as you're streamlining your entourage, pare down the number of stores you visit to only a few each day. You deserve a relaxed approach.

Heirloom Dresses

Especially in generations past, many women painstakingly preserved their wedding dress in the hopes of handing it down to a daughter or granddaughter. If you're gifted a vintage dress or ring that doesn't suit your personal style, it can be a delicate matter to graciously decline the offer without seeming to disrespect family tradition. Here's how one Savvy Bride handled it:

My mother's dress looked gorgeous on her, but I dreaded that she would offer it to me. It was high-collar lace, and so poufy I could fit my entire class of first-graders under the skirt in a sudden downpour. Then it came: why don't I wear hers? I tried it on to please her; I looked like I was wearing a giant lace doily. I gently said I loved it, but it didn't feel right. I'm the only daughter, so it's not like another sister might adopt it. I "insisted" on taking part of the train to make a drawstring bag, which I carried on the day; she was pleased with that. And we'll use the material again for a christening gown—that idea really made a difference! —J.B., LONDON

BRIDAL VOCAB: SPEAKING A NEW LANGUAGE

Do you speak fluent Bride? You might already feel as if you've landed in a new country. Boutonnières? Bomboniere? Balconette bras for your wedding trousseau? (Traditionally, a "trousseau" referred to the collection of linens and clothes accumulated by a young bride for her new home. More recently, it can refer to her collection of honeymoon lingerie.) Wedding Land comes with a language all its own, perhaps none more so than the vocabulary in reference to a wedding dress. Here's an overview, from top to toe.

Fabrics

A hundred shades of white? White, off-white, ivory, champagne, silk white, and diamond white are just some of the hues you may encounter.

Don't be daunted; it's fun to try on different fabrics or simply drape a piece across you. Sooner or later, the Goldilocks approach works: one will seem too stark and wash you out, another will be too creamy, and—you guessed it—one will be just right. Then we get into silks, satins, laces, organzas. . . . You needn't be overwhelmed; the delight is in the trying!

Global Glimpses

Some **Brazilian** brides follow the custom of writing the names of single friends on a slip of paper, and tucking it inside their wedding dress. This is said to bring the ladies good luck in finding a loving partner.

Veils

A confession: I don't know why a bride would sidestep a veil. Truly, how many times in life do you get to wear one? Stacey L. confides that she didn't wear a veil and regretted it for years. Case in point: she incorporated one in every Halloween costume for three years in a row. Go glam, not ghoul. Here's a quick guide:

- **Cocktail length (aka birdcage veil)**: A spray of netting that goes only as far as the chin. Aside from brides, these veils are often used to dramatic and comical effect in soap operas whenever a surprise witness is called in a courtroom climax. According to Karen Willis Holmes, longer styles tend to favor tulle over netting.

- **Shoulder length** (~20 inches long): A lovely choice if you wish to showcase a dress with detail to the lower back or waist. After all, your guests will likely be watching you from behind during the service!

- **Elbow length** (~25 inches long): Falls to your elbow and highlights full-skirted dresses.

- **Waist length** (~30 inches long): A beautiful feature for dresses without trains.

- **Fingertip length** (~36 inches long): One of the most popular lengths for good reason: it complements a wide range of dresses, from vintage to trendy.

- **Knee length** (~45 inches long): Surprise, surprise—this length reaches to your knees! Works well with 1950s-inspired dresses that end at the mid-calf.

- **Ballet length** (depends on the bride's height!): Gently skims the floor. Adds a touch of flair to full-length dresses without trains.

- **Chapel length** (~90 inches long): Shorter than cathedral length, but no less dramatic. We often see them paired with dresses that boast a gorgeous train.

- **Cathedral length** (~120 inches long): The grande dame of veils, as she is the longest and most formal. Reserved for classic, detailed gowns, this style is enjoying high demand at the moment. Willis Holmes advises that this veil typically features several layers, with a "blush" tier (~24 inches) to cover the face.

Heavenly Headdresses

Tiaras and headbands and wreaths, oh my! Savvy Brides have a wonderful array of headdresses to choose from. Or you might prefer a spray of fresh or silk flowers instead. Barrettes are also making a comeback. Both look elegant and will keep the hair off your face and in place for photos.

Global Glimpses

Rather than a veil, a **Japanese** bride dons a headpiece known as a *tsuno-kakushi*. It can variously be a hat, a piece of cloth, or a hood, said to cover her "horns of jealousy." Its purpose is to hide traits such as ego or distrust, characteristics unbecoming of a bride. Some also believe that the horns of jealousy represent the bride's feelings toward her new mother-in-law, with whom she must now compete for her husband's attention. In that case, choosing to cover them denotes her willingness to be an obedient wife.

Necklines

♦ **Bateau (or boat neck):** This style, with sleeves perched high on the upper arm, is enjoying a revival at present. Can also describe a neckline that is straight across the collarbone. Very Audrey Hepburn!

♦ **Cowl:** Soft folds of fabric fall in a U shape (can also be used for the back of the dress).

♦ **Queen Anne:** A "cutout" diamond shape.

♦ **Off-the-shoulder:** Gown sits below the shoulders.

♦ **Sweetheart:** Dips to a heart shape with various degrees of va-va-voom. Brides can choose from girl-next-door to vixen. Willis Holmes says the sweetheart is the most popular and flattering neckline for brides, which explains why it endures.

♦ **Strapless:** Can skim the chest straight across, again with varying degrees of cheekiness.

♦ **Illusion:** Picture a sweetheart or strapless neckline for the main gown, overlaid with a sheer fabric, extending to perhaps a boat neck or rounded crew neckline.

♦ **Surplice:** Fabric is overlaid in a diagonal fashion for a wraplike effect.

♦ **Halter:** Straps of varying thickness extend upward from the bodice in an inverted V.

♦ **V neck:** Features a V shape. Like the sweetheart, it can dip to varying degrees.

♦ **High neck:** Extends up the throat.

Sleeves

Alas, not all of us are comfortable exposing our upper arms, and here a well-chosen sleeve provides elegance and camouflage. Flick through some bridal magazines or go online to check out your options; you'll find a gorgeous variety awaits. Sleeves can be short and capped, mid-length, three-quarter length, or full. They can feature opaque fabric or delicate peekaboo lace. You might prefer a bolero jacket (think: short, fitted jacket favored by Spanish bullfighters), a delicate wrap or shrug that encases your shoulders—or even a cape!

Waists

Wedding dresses showcase just how fluid a waist can be: from the on-high fitting of an empire waist just below the chest, to a drop waist reminiscent of a 1920s flapper. You can almost see the gangsters and speakeasies! Some brides may find the tiny waist and billowing skirt of an A-line to be both flattering and comfortable, while others will cut a slinky figure in a body-conscious sheath or mermaid silhouette, which flares above the knee, not below.

OTHER DRESS-RELATED DECISIONS

Now that you've picked up some bridal lingo and started thinking about the type of gown you want, here are a few additional tips on making your purchase and completing your ensemble.

Using a Dressmaker or Having Alterations Made

Perhaps you'll decide to have your dress made. Take pictures of what you're after and be clear on what you want. Check that your dressmaker will make a trial dress in cotton or muslin first. This is a must.

Other brides might buy a dress off the rack or online, and then have alterations done. Some tips if you take this route:

Buy a size as close to your own as possible; don't be tempted to buy a much bigger dress that is heavily reduced in price, and assume it can be pared down. While it's true that it's easier to take in a dress than to let it out, whittling down billowing fabric to a body-conscious design can take more time and money than you would think.

And I mean this more gently than typed words can convey: Oh beautiful bride, please be realistic about how much weight you want to lose, can lose, or even should lose before the big day. Buying an "incentive size" in hopes it will kickstart a fitness regimen is a surefire way to heap pressure on yourself at what should be a happy (if cheerfully chaotic) time.

If you're ordering a dress online or at a local store, follow up with an email of your exact measurements ("Just to confirm, here are the measurements and style we discussed. . . .") and then copy yourself on it. It will help to have that record in the event they order the wrong size or style. Relying on a phone call can be disastrous: background noise, a poor connection, or a measurement simply misheard can be an expensive error.

It's very gracious not to smoke immediately before a dress fitting or to wear heavy perfume. You'll be in close proximity to the tailor, and you also won't want those strong odors to infuse the material. Or make her pass out.

Renting a Dress

Jon and I had two ceremonies: a legal wedding on a small cliff top overlooking the ocean, followed later by a traditional church wedding. For the second ceremony, I borrowed a gorgeous dress and transformed it with a veil (the previous bride had looked elegant with a spray of flowers in her hair).

Rentals are another cost-effective option. Just keep in mind that alterations may not be possible or, at least, may be very limited, so you should be delighted with your choice of dress as is. And, while each dress will be carefully cleaned on return, it's worth asking if the last bride was a smoker. Some stores will keep a record of that.

Accessories

If you're not using a family member's veil as your "something borrowed," you might find it handy to buy the veil at the same store as your dress, to more easily find one that complements the style. Brides on a tight budget will find accessories such as gloves, garters, and drawstring accessory bags online.

Shapewear

All hail shapewear! Every bride wants a smooth silhouette, and unless you live at the gym, shapewear is the secret to getting one. It will help control any jiggly areas, cinch you in at the waist, and lift your décolletage in a way that will inspire songs and serenades.

Take any foundation garments with you when you go dress shopping. Remember to wear a strapless bra if you have your heart set on a strapless dress. You'll get a much better idea of your silhouette with the right lingerie. If you're blessed with curves, consider having a bra or shapewear sewn into your dress; that way, you won't be worrying about things slipping down or riding up. And while a corset-like effect is wonderful, you can have too much of a good thing. Perhaps sidestep the urge to wear one layer on top of the other: you deserve to enjoy your wedding in comfort.

Technically, shapewear forms part of your bridal trousseau, though today the word typically conjures more frothy, less structured lingerie. You will find an entirely creative selection in stores and online, from delicate to racy to red-light.

Shoes

Another joyously gorgeous item to shop for! All I'd add is this: try to wear them in a little before the big day (slip on some hiking socks and wear the shoes around the house—not glam, but your toes will thank you). Or use gel inserts for a cool and comfortable solution. Finally, give someone a spare pair to bring along, in case it all gets too much. You deserve to be floating with joy, not wincing on the dance floor or through the photos!

Global Glimpses

Though they may wear a white gown, many **Mexican** brides discreetly inject a little color in their wedding attire. By sewing three ribbons to their underwear, they help ensure a happy marriage: yellow to court prosperity, blue to spark good financial luck, and red to guarantee a passionate union. These colors are also associated with New Year celebrations; after all, a wedding also symbolizes a new start.

HAIR AND MAKEUP ARTISTS

The most beautiful brides look polished, lovely, and glowing (as if lit from within). A makeup artist should bring out your natural beauty. This is likely not the time to experiment with a look wildly different from your usual one, as it will look and feel like a mask—think kissable, not Kabuki.

A Savvy Bride books a trial appointment with hair and makeup artists, and takes along a picture of her dress. If staff can see the style and neckline, they will be better able to advise you on something that complements your overall look.

Preparing Your Skin

Ideally, visit a dermatologist six months to a year before your wedding. Your doctor can thoroughly assess your skin and advise a regimen to ensure you'll be glowing. Microdermabrasion and other lunchtime options might need a series of treatments to bring out the best results.

And, to be sure, a Savvy Bride drinks plenty of water, uses sun protection, and aims for eight hours of sleep each night. Okay, that last one is not always possible, but it's a great goal! You'll also be nurturing habits that will reap benefits far beyond your ceremony.

Nails

You can choose from every color in the rainbow, but a simple French manicure looks effortlessly chic. Its neutral palette also keeps the focus on your face, dress, and ring rather than distracting from them.

SOMETHING OLD, SOMETHING NEW . . .

Soledad T. shares that in Guayaquil, Ecuador, brides from well-to-do families borrow their grandmother's diamond earrings for their wedding day—never her pearls, as they symbolize tears.

These brides found touching, personal ways to incorporate something borrowed (or inherited):

I wore my mother's watch, presented to her by her own parents on her wedding day. She passed away when I was six; I took a quiet moment to close my eyes and picture them all with me.　　　　　　　　　　—MIRIAM, GLASGOW

Global Glimpses

In traditional **Japanese** rituals, a bride paints her face and body in white to symbolize purity. She wears a white silk kimono, often featuring exquisite embroidery or other embellishment. Japanese brides have quite a few costume changes during the reception, first changing into a red kimono and then later into a Western-style dress. The couple's union is sealed when they take their first sip of *sake* (rice wine) together.

As an **Indian** wedding approaches, the bride is treated to a ladies-only *mehndi* party, in which they decorate their hands and feet with temporary designs made from henna, a type of plant dye. *Mehndi* designs, often incorporating the groom's initials, are extraordinarily intricate and take hours to apply. Throughout this, the bride must patiently wait for the plant paste to dry as it stains her skin. Loved ones wait on her while she's being adorned and has to sit still.

Then, on the morning of the wedding, both the Indian bride and groom are blessed with a *haldi* ceremony. *Haldi* is yellow turmeric paste that holds both spiritual significance and curative properties. With this in mind, it is applied to the face, legs, arms, and feet. The ritual is said to ward off evil and therefore protects the couple as they begin their life together.

My grandmother's lace handkerchief was in my little bag with lipstick and powder. Maybe it was my imagination, but I was sure it still had her delicate lavender scent. —LUPITA, MEXICO CITY

A pinkie ring from my childhood best friend. Probably unusual, because you don't want something to upstage your wedding ring, but I looked at my hand, and there was my past and my future. —MARLENE, BRUGES

My favorite aunt never had children, and she was really keen for me to wear her best brooch. It wasn't really my taste, but then someone suggested I pin it to the ribbon around my bouquet. Perfect! —KARLA, JOHANNESBURG

BRIDAL BOOT CAMPS

You might be tempted to go on a diet in anticipation of walking up the aisle, but this is the time to be gentle to yourself. Harsh, last-minute cleanses and fad diets will leave you drained, stressed, and much less able to enjoy this happy chapter. Bridal boot camps are popular ways to prep, and if that approach appeals to you, try to see it as a healthy way to let off some steam rather than a pressured way to peel off the pounds.

Kathy Laucius (thetimeisnowfitness.com) is a high-profile and well-respected personal trainer in Houston. Follow her fitness tips to look and feel your best:

♦ Don't wait till the last minute to get in shape. Although you may be tempted to spend the months before the wedding worrying more about the flowers, understand that losing weight doesn't happen overnight.

♦ Do it the right way. Avoid fad diets that leave you lethargic and unhealthy. Simple tweaks such as cutting out processed food, eating whole grains, fruits, and vegetables, and drinking plenty of water are enough to make a change.

♦ Water, water, water. With all the planning and schedules, it's easy to get dehydrated, which will leave you feeling hungry and more likely to make poor food choices, especially when on the go.

♦ Have a plan. If you know you will be attending appointments, have a healthy meal first or take a snack with you.

♦ Lift weights for a toned and sculpted upper body to rock that dress. You don't have to go heavy!

♦ Get your rest. The wedding will be here before you know it.

Global Glimpses

Not every culture is obsessed with a slim bride. In **Mauritania**, girls are dispatched to "fat farms" before their wedding to pile on the pounds. If a bride has stomach rolls, stretch marks, and overlapping thighs (who knew chafing was chic?), it signals her husband is wealthy enough to keep her appetite satisfied.

PART IV

Let's Celebrate!

Chapter Ten

THE CEREMONY

⊗⊗

W E'VE EXPLORED SOME OF THE major choices you face when selecting a location or venue for your wedding. Before making a final
decision, a Savvy Bride researches any required permits or policies that
may affect plans for the ceremony. For example, some places forbid the
throwing of rice or confetti, while others ban the use of flash photography. In my own case, it was easier to ask forgiveness than permission. I
didn't tell Father Patrick that my bridesmaids would be wearing black,
halter-neck dresses with bare shoulders (though that's nothing com-
pared to the skin flashed nowadays). Nor did I mention that we had
decided to forgo the traditional wedding march in favor of Bette Midler
belting out one of her hits. Father Patrick didn't live much longer after
our wedding; I secretly wondered if we led him to an early grave.

You may also want to research the venue's flexibility on start and
finish times. While it's traditional for a bride to arrive a little late, some
heavily booked places won't bend and will cut your ceremony short,
as they'll be starting another one at the top of the hour. Be clear on
time frames.

THE MUST-HAVES

Whatever your choice, the ceremony must have a few indispensable elements: it needs to be legally binding (despite what's depicted in many TV
comedies or big-screen rom-coms, your roommate's online ordination as
minister may not qualify); and, once performed, it needs to be registered.

Global Glimpses

In days of yore, **Cajun** communities in rural outposts could wait months for a visiting official to sanction a matrimonial ceremony. Instead, a betrothed couple would ceremoniously jump over a broom to herald their union, often accompanied by drum beats. This ritual was adopted by **African Americans**, as slaves were often not permitted to marry. The **Romani** (or Roma) people of the United Kingdom also practice the jumping of the broom.

THE ORDER OF SERVICE

The Wedding Order of Service booklet is often completed as a DIY project. It lays out the format of the ceremony and sometimes the reception. It also broadly explains any religious elements or traditions and identifies who will be giving readings. This is especially helpful for those not familiar with the particular religion. An inclusive wedding is a joyous wedding.

TRIAL THE AISLE

The aisle makes an impact on a bride's entrance. Is it long enough to glide up with full drama? Or is it stumpy and short, so the scene you've imagined in your mind for years is covered in barely three steps? After all, you can't do laps! A Savvy Bride considers the physical aspects of the aisle in the place of worship and plans accordingly.

SEATING

In Christian weddings, the bride's family and friends are usually seated to the left, and the groom's to the right. That said, ushers should invite guests to sit on either side if, say, the bride's family consists of only a handful of people who have flown in from overseas, or they're all in witness protection. Jewish weddings are just the opposite in terms of seating. In Orthodox synagogues and in mosques, the genders are separated.

~ Global Glimpses

In **Ecuador**, the oldest relatives are seated in the front row. This is a sign of respect to them as matriarchs and patriarchs. It is also a sign that each family has accepted the other and its history. This blesses the union moving forward.

Fancy taking your vows with several thousand other brides and grooms? **South Korea** is a hub for weddings on a mass scale. Each year, thousands of couples, all followers of the Unification Church and its now-deceased founder, Reverend Sun Myung Moon, are joined in matrimony. Also known as "Moonies," these adherents often meet their intended (selected by the church) only days before the service. They file into stadiums filled with other couples, with no room for relatives and friends.

YOUR BACKDROP OR OVERHEAD

Perhaps you're thinking about pledging your vows in an outdoor garden under a floral archway, or against the backdrop of a beach, or on a rooftop looking over a city skyline. Then there's a chuppah, a traditional Jewish wedding canopy, which can take many forms.

There are no set rules as to how a chuppah should be constructed—the idea is to have four poles with a piece of fabric mounted on top. Sometimes a prayer shawl is used, or a white cloth symbolizing purity.

We asked friends and family to contribute to our chuppah by having them each create a design on a white piece of fabric so that we would be surrounded by them during the ceremony and always. My mom sewed all the squares together in what ended up being a giant undertaking.

Mom and I arranged the squares, and we also added photos of our four sets of grandparents so that they would be looking down on us from above. We chose a blue material for the reverse side of the chuppah—reminiscent of the sky.

The last part was to figure out how to suspend the chuppah from the bamboo poles. Mom suggested a series of circles that would fit around the poles. She used wool from sweaters that her own mom had made years earlier to wrap the rings so that we had my grandma with us too.

—TIRZA K., BOGOTÁ

INTERFAITH CEREMONIES

Are you considering an interfaith or interdenominational wedding? If so, of course you could choose one house of worship or the other, or select a venue that is entirely neutral. The latter option can help keep the "civil" in civil weddings should tempers run. You might select ceremonial elements that incorporate both faiths (if indeed both parties have faiths) or stay with secular vows, readings, and songs. An Order of Service will be especially welcome in a blended ceremony, to better explain parts of the service and to be more inclusive of guests. Unity candles can provide a touching underscore.

Global Glimpses

The **Uighur** (also spelled Uyghur or Yugur) people of China have a custom of the groom shooting three arrows (thankfully, with no arrowheads) at his bride. He is called on during the ceremony to break the arrows and the bow. This symbolizes commitment to a union marked by longevity and love.

The breaking of the glass in **Jewish** weddings has various origins. At the end of the ceremony, the groom wraps a glass in a cloth napkin and crushes it underfoot. Some say that this act symbolizes the destruction of the great Temple of Jerusalem in the year 70, while others believe that the shards remind us that moments of jubilation should be tempered with a little reality. Either way, the ritual concludes with guests shouting "mazel tov!" (good luck!) at the sound of the glass shattering.

According to **Zulu** tradition, the groom's family slaughters a cow to welcome their new daughter. The lady of the hour then places money inside the cow's stomach to symbolize that she is now a full-fledged member of the family.

In the **Maasai** community of Kenya, the father of the bride spits on her head and décolletage to shower blessings upon her. Tradition dictates that she then leave with her groom and not look back lest she turn to stone. **Greek** superstition in years past also held that (dry) spitting in the bride's direction offers her protection from evil spirits.

Immediately following a ceremony in **Sri Lanka**, it is customary for the bride and groom to honor both sets of parents by lying flat on the ground in front of them as a sign of respect. They also present their parents with gifts, with clothing being a common choice for the mothers.

Chapter Eleven

THE RECEPTION

❧

THE CEREMONY WILL BE BEAUTIFUL and touching. Now it's time to kick up the celebrations at the reception!

By the time the couple have left for their honeymoon, guests will remember only a few things about the wedding: whether the bride and groom were glowing or stressed, and whether they enjoyed the food, drinks, and music. Joy and abundance is the theme of the day.

Provide your guests with a cascade of treats to nibble on: I've been to champagne-and-cake ceremonies that were lovely. Less lovely was joining most of the wedding guests in all our finery to chow down at the nearest fast-food place afterward. A Savvy Couple ensures their guests won't be scrambling for a drive-thru to assuage their hunger. Ask your caterer to place lids on the trays of canapés; this simple strategy means wait staff can reach deeper into the crowd before all the finger food is gone.

GENERAL FORMAT

Many receptions begin with the traditional receiving line. This is where the newlyweds, their parents, and the bridal party welcome guests. The line begins with whomever is hosting the reception and usually follows this order: bride's parents, groom's parents, happy couple, and then core members of the bridal party (maid/matron of honor and best man as a minimum; others also include bridesmaids and groomsmen; flower girls and ring bearers are excused). Or you might choose to have everyone gather to enjoy canapés while you finish taking your wedding photos. Invite them to be seated and then stand to welcome the bridal party.

In general, receptions tend to include some or all of the following elements, with the format varying to suit the circumstances:

◆ Appetizers (hors d'oeuvres, canapés, etc.)

◆ Entrées (with toasts to the newlyweds in between)

◆ Toasts (and while the mood is relaxed and festive, it's not a good idea to serve minors alcohol, even at a reception at your home; you can be held legally responsible if they get behind the wheel or otherwise cause mayhem while under the influence)

◆ Dancing, kicked off by the bride and groom, followed by their parents

◆ The party itself!

◆ Cake cutting (you can release the photographer/videographer earlier if this is done before or soon after the bridal dance)

◆ Cleaning up (for self-catered events)

◆ Departure and farewell: Guests may be asked to assemble at the entrance to the hall or to form an arch for a send-off. Sometimes sparklers are handed out, and guests hold them up to form a tunnel through which the couple runs as they leave for their hotel or honeymoon. Others ask the guests to form a circle, with the happy couple moving around in opposite directions to bid each person farewell.

CHOOSING AN EMCEE

Many DJs will agree to serve as master of ceremonies, but this is a role that deserves its own dedicated person. Accord a trusted friend or relative this honor and responsibility.

The job of an emcee is to keep things moving, keep the party going, and also to be the go-to person for photographers and other staff. This host will need to introduce him- or herself to the staff at the event, and be ready to pitch in when problems arise. Don't feel obliged to pick a comedian; it's much more about sincerity than being a Vegas headliner. Good emcees will be mindful of the time schedule. They will introduce

⁓ Global Glimpses

Any volunteers for a human carpet? In some islands of **French Polynesia**, the wedding reception wraps up with relatives of the bride lying face-down on the floor (or in the dirt) so that the couple can walk over them. This underscores the royal treatment of the newlyweds, and protects them as they cross the threshold into married life. You've probably had occasion to crank up the party and "get down!"—but not quite like this.

---

speakers, let people know when (and where) to start the buffet line and when to join the dancing, and ask everyone to stand and greet the couple as they enter.

SEATING

The bridal table consists of the couple and their adult attendants. Sometimes their parents join the bride and groom, but usually they host their own tables. In the case of divorce or separation, each parent hosts his or her own table, equally prominent in proximity to the bridal party. It's a good idea not to push the envelope too much, as even on happy occasions, civility can have its limits.

Place the officiant and his or her spouse at one of the front tables rather than at the back near the clanging kitchen or in the path of restroom traffic. Invite them to say grace if you would like the meal blessed. If you're concerned about shielding them from improprieties, plant someone neutral at the table as a buffer to any controversial conversation along religious or political lines. Don't place grown-up guests at a children's table, but do consider enlisting an older teen cousin or two to keep an eye on the little ones.

TRADITIONS

Customs abound as to who will get married next. The tossing of the bouquet (and its masculine counterpart, the garter toss) is time honored, and brides can choose various times and settings to perform the ritual. Just temper creativity with a little caution. One couple in Europe caused a plane to crash because they wanted to perform the tradition from on high. They had hired a light aircraft to head to their honeymoon, and planned to toss the bouquet upon their aerial exit. The flowers got caught in the plane's engine and sparked a small fire, causing the aircraft to nose-dive into a building.

◯ TIP:

Set up a gift table near the entry. Many people will buy from the gift registry and have it delivered to the RSVP address, but there will always be someone who arrives with parcel in hand. It's much more gracious to have a pretty area in which to store gifts rather than a corner on the floor.

After our ceremony, we had the ritual "fishing for the ring," called jua-jui. A large bowl was placed in front of us. It was filled with milk from ornate jugs, and then many almonds and coins were added. Finally, my wedding ring was dropped in! My husband and I playfully pushed back and forth to find the ring first, feeling our way through the ingredients and splashing the milk. I was allowed to use both hands, while my husband was allowed to use only one. Many rounds of this fun and messy game were played with the whole family cheering us both. Whoever finds the ring will enjoy the upper hand in marriage.

— RASHMI SINGHVI, HOUSTON, TEXAS (who isn't telling who won)

◯ Global Glimpses

Other cultures have their own take on the bouquet toss. In **Finland**, the bride is blindfolded, and her single friends dance around her. She playfully grabs for them, and they keep her guessing by slipping out of her grasp. She eventually clutches a guest, and places her tiara or headdress on her captive. This lady will be the next to marry!

Not to be outdone, a groom in **Estonia** is also blindfolded on the dance floor and has to place his top hat on a guest—effectively crowning the next man to stand in his place!

CATERED VERSUS SELF-CATERED

It can be very tempting and cost effective to have friends or relatives do the cooking and serving. But really, do you want your favorite aunts and cousins slaving away in the kitchen, or celebrating with you? It's much more fun to be dancing, not scrubbing pots before the community center has to be closed.

WEIGHING YOUR FOOD OPTIONS

Are you considering a sit-down dinner or a buffet? A mixture of both? I've seen weddings where salad and bread were already at the table, with a buffet for the main course. If a buffet is chosen, the bride and groom should still be served a selection of dishes at the table: as the happy couple, this is your day to be waited on! Or perhaps you want to limit the food service to lighter fare? Here's a rundown of the pros and cons of the different options.

Buffet

 ♦ **Pros:** A buffet is more casual, and seamlessly allows for more mixing between guests. It's also more economical than a sit-down dinner. A variety of dishes means different tastes are more easily accommodated, as well as dietary restrictions.

 ♦ **Cons:** It's less formal, and you might want something more elegant, or want your guests to be served rather than having to help themselves.

Sit-Down Dinner

 ♦ **Pros:** This option is more elegant, with guests served at their table. There is no crowding around buffet tables. It can be more time efficient, as toasts are made between courses. Some couples feel this moves along the reception more smoothly, and avoids the buffet dilemma of having some people up and others seated while toasts are being made.

 ♦ **Cons:** It tends to be more expensive, with less choice of dishes (though certainly enough).

Cocktails and Light Fare

♦ **Pros:** Cocktail receptions are relaxed and allow good mingling and time with your guests. Finger food is festive and generally more economical than a formal meal. This option is also shorter in duration, so you can keep costs down across the board: the venue, an open bar, the music. Resist the urge to offer spirits for a small charge; better to have a more modest drinks menu that is fully complementary.

♦ **Cons:** You might like something longer and more involved. Long-distance guests and other out-of-towners might expect a meal.

Another consideration is how many wait staff to hire. Some base this decision on a desired ratio of staff to guests. Consider whether you'll need a bartender or a coat-check person. Depending on your catering arrangement, you may have to tip staff individually, or a blanket gratuity may be included in the contract. How will the staff be dressed? Will they be hired through caterers or separately through an agency, or will you be obligated to use the venue's event staff? Check whether you will need public liability insurance in the event of staff or guests injuring themselves.

Offering some meat-free options is a good idea. Even if no one on your list is a strict vegetarian, some health-conscious guests might prefer the choice or might bring along someone who is.

TIP:

Bomboniere are weddings favors given to guests. Candies, candles, and small picture frames are popular mementos of the day. How about personalized USB (flash) drives, boxed gourmet tea bags, or playing cards with a photo of the bride and groom?

WEDDING FAVORS

We've likely all seen the candy-coated almonds handed out at weddings or bedecking the tables. They're a lovely tradition, signifying the bitter and sweet of life. But I noticed a practical wedding touch that proved very popular at a garden reception: staff held baskets filled with a variety of clear plastic heel protectors for the ladies' shoes. As they stepped from the terrace to the lawn, their heels didn't get stained with grass or sink into soft earth. (If you can't afford to provide them, you might suggest on your wedding website that guests bring along a pair.)

A word on the trend of providing gift bags for guests: go ahead if you like, but this is not a conference or expo! You needn't give your guests merchandise samples. But if you insist, keep it sweet and simple.

~ Global Glimpses

After a **Muslim** bride and groom sign their *nikah* (wedding contract), a celebration commences. This reception is known as a *walima*, and the feasting lasts two days. The menu is sure to include rice, fish, and chicken—all symbols of fertility.

Wedding receptions in many cultures feature traditions to help ensure a prosperous start to married life. **Greek** celebrations often include a song during which guests pin cash to the wedding dress. In **Polish** communities, guests happily pay for the privilege of dancing with the bride by donating money, which is collected by a family friend.

Not to be outdone, **French Canadians** often stage a "sock dance" at their wedding receptions. Unmarried siblings of the bride or groom wear funny socks and entertain everyone with a silly dance. Guests throw money at the performers, which is collected for the happy couple.

And in **Germany**, friends and family collaborate to produce a wedding newspaper, brimming with pictures, stories, and funny marriage advice. It is then sold at the reception to help fund the honeymoon.

ALTERNATIVE VENUES

Many couples choose an event facility, restaurant, or hotel for their reception, and for good reason. Others find their dream wedding in a less traditional setting, such as a zoo, museum, or lakeside marquee.

One alternative proving very popular is the home away from home: renting a condo or vacation house for a few days. This lends a casual, homey vibe, without having to see your own home taken over. It also means a more relaxed time to wrap up the festivities at the end of the night, without fear of overtime charges. Check out vacation rentals online to spark your imagination for romantic settings.

Chapter Twelve

THE CAKE

〰️

THE WEDDING CAKE IS A BEAUTIFUL, elegant, and delicious tradition. That said, you can take complete leeway in how you'd like to embrace this sweet concoction: the style, the flavors, and the timing of the cutting are just a few of the ways in which you can stamp your personal style on the ritual. Maybe you're leaning toward a simple, time-honored recipe, or a delightful croquembouche—a French wedding-cake tower. How about a vanilla cake with a chocolate fountain pouring over the top? Or a cascade of red velvet cupcakes?

Here are some ideas to get you started. Whatever you choose, the cake should complement the general theme of your wedding. Depending on your budget, it can be the sole dessert, or the centerpiece to a dessert menu, or the finale to your event, served with coffee.

- ♦ **Traditional:** If you're seeking a classic touch, the traditional Western wedding cake is fruit cake coated in white marzipan. It offers a rich, full flavor. The alcohol content means it lasts well; the top tier is often stored in the freezer and enjoyed on the couple's first anniversary or saved for their first baby's christening.

- ♦ **Croquembouche:** Pronounced "crokem-boosh," this traditional French wedding cake is whimsical, elegant, and a decoration all its own. Profiteroles (balls of choux pastry) are filled with cream or custard, then dipped in chocolate sauce or encased in spun toffee, and stacked in a cone-shaped tower.

- **Cupcake Towers:** Artfully arranged stacks of cupcakes or similar individual portions can look fabulous, cheerful, and colorful. And with no need to cut, serving is a breeze.

- **Le Fake Cake:** Some brides prefer this option, as a few faux layers preserve the dramatic statement of a larger cake while being more economical. Another approach is to order a small wedding cake for display, along with a sheet cake made by the same baker, which is kept in the kitchen. This can be a sound, budget-conscious choice. Beware, though: some specialty bakers decline to take orders that pair their creation with a store-bought sheet cake, as the quality will likely be different.

- **Simple Sponge:** You might also opt for a simple but beautifully decorated sponge cake, which can be dressed up further with berries and cream to create a stunning, seasonal dessert. Both elegant and economical.

Global Glimpses

In **Peru**, wedding cakes hold a sweet promise of romance beyond the happy couple. Charms are threaded onto ribbons and then slipped between the layers of wedding cake. Before the cake is cut, single ladies are invited to tug gently on the ribbon of their choice. One ribbon has a faux wedding ring attached. This lucky guest is said to be the next bride!

Meanwhile, couples in **Bermuda** are presented with his and her wedding cakes. Ivy often entwines the two desserts (symbolizing love); in addition, the bride's version is topped with a cedar sapling (to help ensure a shared life of longevity and happiness). The newlyweds then plant the sapling at their home to watch it take root and flourish—much like their union.

PLEASE, OH PLEASE: NO CAKE FIGHTS!

For decades, couples cut the cake and fed each other the first slice. Charming idea. Unfortunately, someone, somewhere, started a cake fight. Personally, I'd like to fly back in time, slap them, and fly back. This practice mystifies me! I love funny moments at weddings as much as the next girl, but why is it considered witty for a bride and groom to smash each other with cake? And what bride wants her makeup and dress smeared? Again, it's mystifying, but if you insist, I shall step back (and away from the flying frosting) and concede with a smile, "It's your day."

CHOOSING A BAKER OR CAKE DECORATOR

A Savvy Bride starts looking at wedding cakes *at least* six months beforehand; as with many professions, the best wedding cake vendors are booked far in advance. Enjoy looking at ideas online or in magazines, and take along your favorites to a few specialty bakeries (or email them initially for a rough quote, with links to your favorites). The bakery will need to know your budget and how many servings to provide. It's always handy to go above your actual guest count, for friends or relatives who can't make it. Perhaps some extra for grandma's friends at her nursing home or bridge club? As mentioned, ask about a multilayered cake, as well as the option of a smaller cake for photos, supplemented by a sheet cake for cutting up.

Enjoy a delicious time with taste testing!

PERSONALIZING YOUR CAKE

You might like to add personalized decorative elements, such as initials for you and your intended. Perhaps soft daisies to complement the ones sprinkled on your invitations and woven through your hair? Was there an element from your parents' or grandparents' cakes that you would like to see echoed in yours? This is a subtle, loving way to incorporate an intergenerational touch and pay homage to your heritage.

One couple, avid scuba divers, personalized their cake with motifs of underwater creatures dotted about. The bride's sister went strictly classic the following year, with three tiers of white marzipan, each layer encircled by black velvet ribbon—simple and striking! An international couple chose self-patterned symbols from each of their countries.

⟶ Global Glimpses

In **West Africa**, cowrie shells represent fertility and prosperity. This explains their popularity in wedding decorations and cake designs.

Cake Toppers

Many choose to top the cake with figurines of the bridal couple, which today might be bride/groom, bride/bride, or groom/groom. Whatever the combination, they're easy to find online and lend a festive touch.

DELIVERY

You might be tempted to ask a friend or relative to pick up the cake to save on delivery charges, but I encourage you to "go pro." Professional bakers will have proper vans, or will contract couriers who do, and you'll want it properly outfitted and temperature controlled. Chances are a well-meaning friend or relative won't be familiar with the best ways to transport your delicate cake, and that goes beyond driving slowly and trying not to brake suddenly!

CUTTING AND SERVING

Decide who will cut and distribute the cake. The staff at the event may charge an extra fee per slice, sometimes known as "cakeage" (like corkage), which can quickly add up, so you might like to ask a friend or some favorite aunts to oversee this. And consider how you'd like the cake to be presented: laid on platters, or placed in little bags for guests to take home if they wish? After all, there's always the tradition of young ladies placing a slice of wedding cake under their pillow, to dream of their future husband!

Global Glimpses

Norwegian and Danish receptions traditionally feature a *kransekake* (or *kransekage*), meaning "wreath cake" or "doughnut cake." Delicious rings of ground almond are baked and set atop one another, with the smallest at the apex (saved for the newlyweds).

Instead of cake, **Indian** newlyweds partake of five tastes of a sweet dish, *panchamrutham* (from *panch* meaning "five" and *amrutha* signifying "nectar of immortality"). Among its sweet ingredients are milk (for piety), yogurt (connoting progeny), honey (inspiring sweet words), and ghee, a clarified butter (representing victory). It is considered the milk of the gods, and in fact, at different times of the year, idols are bathed in this mixture and finally immersed in water (purity). Couples also share yellow rice (*pulihora*) during the ceremony. The coloring comes from the spice turmeric, revered for its spiritual role and for symbolizing prosperity.

"Tasting the Four Elements" is a **Yoruba (Nigerian)** ritual equally rich in flavor and significance. Newlyweds sample four flavors that represent a relationship's ups and downs: sour (lemon) signifies rejection or hardship; bitter (vinegar) represents disappointment; hot (cayenne) underscores a passionate union; and finally the ceremony culminates in sweet notes (honey). This ritual symbolizes the couple's commitment to navigate the tough times in their marriage and appreciate the bright spots.

PART V

Touches That Transform

Chapter Thirteen

MUSIC

❧

FROM THE BEAUTIFUL STRAINS OF classical music as you glide up the aisle, to head-banging at the reception, Savvy Couples have a wide variety of tunes to choose from. Music sets the tone more easily and more quickly than almost any other element in a wedding. Gentle background music can welcome guests; later, it can take center stage for the dancing.

You can book a band, a DJ, or a string quartet, or you can keep it simple with a playlist. In fact, a playlist is also good for when a band or DJ takes a break, and it can prove a handy backup in case their equipment fails.

Whichever you choose, meet with your musician or DJ to discuss the type of songs or compositions you would like played. They'll likely suggest a mixture of contemporary and classic tunes, which will be inclusive for guests of all ages.

As we discussed in the chapter on receptions, it's not a good idea to have the DJ double as the emcee, especially if he comes across as a wannabe celebrity.

Our DJ was open to our kind of music (alternative), and we were also happy with sixties music, which always seems to get everyone up on the dance floor. But then he wanted to include a medley of "The Time Warp," "The Bus Stop," and the dreaded "Birdy Dance," which inexplicably resurfaces every few years in an ode to bad taste everywhere. We nixed any dances with actions. He put up a fight, but we stood strong. —MILLIE, HONOLULU, HAWAII

~◦ Global Glimpses

Traditional **Zulu** weddings are energetic, high-tempo celebrations, marked by dance-offs between the families of the bride and groom.

A bridal shuffle? In **Ireland**, the bride's feet must stay on the floor at all times when she and the groom are dancing. If not, it is thought that evil fairies might come to sweep her away.

And while a **Swedish** bride isn't required to shuffle, she might find herself a little uncomfortable dancing: each of her shoes contain a coin. Traditionally, her father places a silver coin in her left shoe, and her mother slips a gold coin in her right shoe. This is said to bestow financial prosperity on their daughter and her new husband.

If a Swedish groom leaves the room for any reason, all the other men at the wedding are allowed to kiss his bride. And if the bride slips out for a moment, guests can take their chances with her new husband!

Chapter Fourteen

FLOWERS

■

YOU MIGHT BE AMUSED TO KNOW that in days past, fresh flowers weren't used primarily for decoration. Instead, they were used to mask body odor, as people often bathed only once a week. Today, their delicate blossoms lend color, fragrance, and romance to all aspects of a wedding.

Flowers might be fresh, silk, or another fabric altogether. In addition to their use in table centerpieces, church altar decorations, buttonholes, and the bridal bouquet, you'll find them adding a note of whimsy and beauty to tiny posies, cheerful garlands, or the bride's flowing tresses. You might choose to marry under a floral arch or use bunches of flowers as pew decorations. While bouquets of mixed colors can be stunning, using a single type and color of flower can lend a striking element.

A Savvy Bride asks at her temple, church, or other venue about contacting her fellow brides who are getting married on the same day. They might be able to share the costs of beautiful and neutral decorations.

An eco-bride might choose silk flowers. And you might just be pleasantly surprised at the range of paper (yes, paper) flowers available today. Banish any thought of stiff, crepe flowers in primary colors; think delicate palettes of beautifully crafted blooms that won't wilt in the heat or fly off in a stiff breeze. They might also avoid this:

We attended a wedding where the bride was stung by a bee that was attracted to her bouquet. Some giddy old aunt went to the kitchen asking the caterers for an onion, cut it in half, and rubbed it on the bride's arm. Needless to say, she stunk for the rest of the evening. —JO-ANNE, MELBOURNE

The bride above might have taken a tip from horticulture schools: including natural insect repellents such as mint or lavender in your bouquet can help deter bugs.

⟲ **TIP:**

A *boutonnière* (French: buttonhole) is a floral adornment for a man's jacket lapel, usually a floral bud or the head of a single flower.

The symbolism of flowers can infuse your bouquet with extra beauty and meaning. That said, don't be too wedded to the meaning (no pun intended). I adore arum lilies and carried a few for our first (legal) wedding, despite the fact they are known as death lilies. Their long, slender stems complemented the column style of our sheath dresses. They later made an appearance at our church ceremony.

AVOIDING POWERFUL SCENTS

Flowers should lend subtle notes of fragrance rather than dominant scents. Overpowering aromas can trigger headaches, migraines, and other negative reactions. It's also worth checking with your florist about whether your bouquets, centerpieces, and church decorations tend to shed a lot of pollen. (Even if you arrange the flowers yourself, your supplier can help with tips.) Excess pollen can trigger allergic reactions and asthma attacks, and stain white fabric.

~ᴑ *Global Glimpses*

Irish brides often tuck a few herbs into their bouquets: a sprig of rose-mary, thyme, even a little garlic are popular inclusions.

In her bouquet, a **Welsh** bride carries myrtle, which Greek mythology has long associated with the goddess Aphrodite. It is a symbol of love, and a bride presents her attendants with a cutting. If the bridesmaid plants the cutting in her yard and it blooms, she will soon marry, says tradition.

Finnish brides are happy to keep the flames of passion burning in their relationship. With this in mind, they often tuck a symbolic match into their bouquet! Other brides sew one into the lining of their wedding gown.

While not strictly a flower, pine cones and branches are often featured at Scandinavian weddings, as they symbolize fertility. **Danish** brides might find the entrance to their family home festooned with a "Gate of Honor" made of pine branches in an arc design.

~ᴑ TIP:

Pledging your vows in a garden or on a lawn? Chat with ground staff about the plants and flowers nearest your area, and how frequently the lawn is mowed. Having it done three days prior could help minimize reaction to grass clippings.

Chapter Fifteen

PHOTOS AND VIDEO

❧

O NE PARTICULAR INDIAN WEDDING stays in my mind for its pomp
and ceremony. We waited in line to congratulate the bride and
groom, who were seated at elaborate thrones. After that, while milling
around, I counted no fewer than six different camera crews, for both
video and still photography. I was intrigued: single girls were being photographed, and their names recorded. Local guests explained these girls
were of marriageable age. At the next wedding, they said, I would find
albums bursting with images. These would be poured over by potential
mothers-in-law, eager to find their son a suitable match.

For most of us, though, wedding photos and video each play a special
role for a more fundamental reason: as your beautiful wedding whizzes
by in a happy blur, they help preserve the story of how your celebration
unfolded. Photos capture the look and feel of the day, whether it's that
first kiss, an adorable flower girl strewing rose petals, or the expression
of misty nostalgia on your parents' faces. (They also unwittingly capture
comical trends in wedding photography: pictures of the couple's faces
imposed over a lake, or in a champagne flute.)

But perhaps my favorite is the video. It means that in years to come,
you can look back to see and hear your younger selves pledging your
love, sharing a laugh, or simply gazing at each other. It's a chance to
watch again as your beloved grandfather makes a touching and dignified
toast, or as the best man bungles his rehearsed speech with a hilarious

gaffe. And your children will be highly amused; without this evidence, they might never believe you were once young.

So charged with those important roles, the photographer and videographer should meet a few key criteria. Let's review some strategies to choosing good people to do the job.

PHOTOGRAPHER

Finding a photographer by word of mouth is a sound strategy, but keep in mind that the feel and outcome you're seeking could be quite different from what your best friend, cousin, or colleague had in mind. You'll want to review the photographer's website, but be sure to view a physical album as well. Though rare, it is possible for a would-be photographer to upload someone else's work as their own. In any case, you'll want to meet any potential candidates in person. And will they have an assistant on the day, to sweep back the bride's hair or check for other elements that need primping?

Once you've seen their site and portfolio, ask about various packages and what is included in each. Must you agree to purchase X dollars' worth of framed or printed photos? Does the photographer offer special effects such as sepia tones? Can you buy the proofs for a flat fee, print the photos, and arrange your own album?

Bring in tear sheets from magazines or send the photographer links to sites with poses you love. Use any visual aids to convey the look and feel you're after. Are you interested in mostly formal shots with a sprinkling of candid shots, or vice versa? It's a good idea to agree on a list of specific images: getting ready at the bride's house/hotel room, getting into the wedding car, arriving at the venue, bridesmaids walking down

---

Global Glimpses

In the **Congo** region of Africa, weddings are somber events, where it is considered disrespectful and even tacky for the couple to appear jovial. To ensure that everything is taken seriously, they are not to smile during or after the ceremony, nor in any of their wedding photos.

---

the aisle, the vows. . . . I couldn't keep a straight face when I was asked to "gaze lovingly at my bouquet" (really!). Then there's cutting the cake and dancing. Besides specific shots, point out anyone special you'd like to be photographed, such as a great-grandparent or young ring bearer, or ask a family member to do so on the day.

If your budget allows, consider hiring the photographer for a trial run by having them take your engagement shots or some portraits. Get a sense of how easy they are to work with, whether they are directive or passive, and whether either of those approaches works for you.

This final point came into focus for me when I needed an author photo for my first book. Let's call it "A Tale of Two Photographers." I booked a seasoned shutterbug with an excellent portfolio; we chatted, and she was lovely. There seemed nothing to be concerned about, yet something nagged at me. On a whim, I contacted a film school in New York City to ask that they post an ad for a final-year photography student or recent graduate to shoot some pictures. I now had two photo shoots booked—extravagant, I know—but I was so glad I did. The photos from the veteran came out stiff and cold: I truly looked like human taxidermy. Or a lab specimen you might find suspended in formaldehyde. The graduate, on the other hand, was relaxed and casual, which made me relaxed in turn. Guess whose shots I used? And I've booked her each year since (if you're reading the print edition, flip to the back of the book to see her work). Kudos, Elizabeth Shrier (elizabethshrier.com)!

⌒◯ TIP:

It's gracious to provide a meal for those who are "working your wedding." It needn't be a multi-course affair with wine pairings (in fact, avoiding alcohol is a good idea lest their services be impaired). A DJ, photographer, and videographer will appreciate a main course and simple dessert, for example, and somewhere to sit briefly. Caterers are used to providing these meals, and if you're self-catering, you can make up plates ahead of time, or simply invite those concerned to join the buffet.

Everyone's a photographer today. Have your emcee invite guests to snap away, but ask that they please consider the professional photographer and videographer, who will both need space to get primary shots. Also, suggest a hashtag that everyone can use when they post your pictures online, so that you can find them all easily.

VIDEOGRAPHER

We have a delightful wedding video, but we were amused that for an entire song, it showed nothing but people chewing. Really—an entire three minutes of people eating. When we asked gently about this, the video guy explained that he wanted to make sure that he captured many of my close relatives. So, to be safe, he basically took close-ups of anyone who looked vaguely Indian, and there they are, captured in all their dining glory: teeth gnashing, jaws flapping, Adam's apples flying up and down in a choreographed dance. It was an anatomy of a meal, certainly in more detail than we bargained for. Lesson learned. We might have pointed out a few close relatives or a frail grandparent for special mention in the video, and let him know we were happy to leave it at that.

A Savvy Couple clarifies that they will own both "raw vision" (meaning unedited footage), as well as the video edited for them. It's a good idea to have two versions cut: a five- to ten-minute capsule of highlights, and a longer, comprehensive video (forty-five to sixty minutes), perhaps with full speeches. Or inquire if you can purchase just the raw version and have it edited later; you'd be surprised how many wedding videos sit on shelves for years, waiting to be watched. You might find delaying this cost to be a welcome financial reprieve. Discuss whether the videographer retains copyright and portfolio rights to display clips of your wedding on their site, and, if so, for how long. Consider whether you're both comfortable with this, and how you'll be identified (usually just first names and state, or perhaps your hometown too).

You might also arrange to include a little surprise or two:

We asked a relative to catch the videographer for a few minutes and to interview our grandparents. It was so touching to see them smiling and doling out wedding advice from a bygone era. It was also a lovely surprise for our parents. Recently, my husband's grandfather passed away, and here was this cherished memento of him recalling early married life after the war.

—AUBREE, MOBILE, ALABAMA

DIY Approach

If your budget is limited, perhaps ask friends if they would each take an hour to do the videotaping. That way, they can help out but still have time to relax and enjoy the day. Be sure to schedule an enthusiastic imbiber early in the evening, before the champagne kicks in.

In sum, your approach to both the photographer and videographer should be "research, question, decide, then release." Don't micromanage once you've chosen vendors and agreed on the menu of crucial wedding shots. Give them space to do what they need and let them know who their contact person will be on the day—and give yourself a break from the worry.

Chapter Sixteen
TRANSPORT

❧

AROUND THE TIME JON AND I were getting married, there was an ad on TV that caught my eye. It featured a couple about to pledge their vows, when the church doors burst open, a man on a motorcycle roars up the aisle, and the bride races off with him. Lest he be too complacent, I teased Jon that I wouldn't enter the church until I heard he was sweating with nerves. Alas, it takes a lot to unsettle him, so I just entered the church the regular way. It's good to keep a man on his toes, though!

How would you like to make your entry and exit? Perhaps a classic vintage Jaguar is your style, or you're charmed by the idea of a sleek limo or horse-drawn carriage. There is so much variety today: bridal parties pour out of bright-red fire trucks and yellow school buses; grooms arrive by helicopter (not so great for a bride's hair) or via speedboat (ditto the hair).

Whichever option you choose, be sure to allow plenty of time to get to the service and again to the reception. It's also a lovely touch for the groomsmen to organize a hamper of drinks and finger food for the bridal party to enjoy while photos are being taken; they will be very welcome between the service and the reception.

PARKING PERMITS FOR HOME RECEPTIONS
A Savvy Bride or Groom checks with the local city or county authorities about parking permits for a home wedding. They're usually inexpensive

and far cheaper than guests getting parking tickets as a memento of your day!

Global Glimpses

Hindu and Muslim cultures celebrate the groom's arrival with a procession known as *baraat*. The man of the hour is resplendent astride a horse, lavishly adorned with beading and plumage. A procession of well-wishers surround him, outfits ablaze in glorious gem colors, often cheering along to the strains of a mobile band as they wind through the streets to the ceremony.

Indian royal weddings inject even more pomp and circumstance, with the groom making his entrance atop an elephant! This spectacular sight is seen occasionally in the US and UK: a few years ago, downtown San Diego ground to a standstill as tourists, drivers, and storekeepers paused to witness this pageantry. A special-event permit was issued, and authorities shut down the local trolley service briefly so as not to spook the majestic creature.

WEDDING SHUTTLES

If your budget allows, providing shuttle buses for your guests is a generous gesture, especially if the location is hard to reach or parking there will be limited. Elderly guests will also appreciate it, as will anyone who would like to enjoy a drink. That said, there is no obligation if this will overstretch your finances; guests will have plenty of notice to make their own plans. Check that the venue's parking lot can accommodate buses and has a ramp for any wheelchair users.

PART VI

Grace with Gifts

Chapter Seventeen

GIFTS

HERE'S A RETRO TRADITION YOU might find quaint: Until about the 1950s, it was common for a girl in her mid- to late teens to be given a hope chest or glory box (also called a "bottom drawer" in the UK). In it, she carefully stored items for her future married life—chiefly household linens and perhaps a special outfit. Sometimes, homewares and other useful items would be given to her for her birthday and other occasions to keep her glory box brimming. When that marriage proposal came, she was ready to take stock of the chest's contents to start her own home.

Today, your wedding guests will likely use online shopping to present you with something for your married life and to commemorate your union.

BRIDAL REGISTRIES: TO HAVE OR HAVE NOT?

Some couples are uncomfortable with registries (as were Jon and I), but in fact, time-pressed guests find it eliminates guesswork and streamlines the process by allowing them to order online and have the gift delivered. It also avoids the three-toaster scenario, common in days past. The main thing to ensure is that guests know the registry is an option, not an expectation; this can be explained discreetly by mothers of the bride and groom, or other close family or friends.

Usually, a department store is chosen for the bridal registry. Wedding planners encourage couples to register four to six months before the day;

any earlier, and products or collections may be discontinued or otherwise no longer stocked. Choose a wide range of goods to reflect different budgets; that said, a few wish-list items can be sprinkled through, as friends or family members will likely band together to buy a group gift (but you should still send them individual thank-you notes).

A Savvy Bride does not include a printout of the gift registry in the same envelope as the invitation. If you have a wedding website, it can be mentioned there.

SPECIALTY STORES

There is a growing trend toward choosing a specialty store instead of a department store, or at least in addition to one. One couple registered with a home improvement warehouse, as everyone knew they had bought a fixer-upper and were going to launch themselves into home renovations instead of jetting off on a honeymoon. Other couples favor camping stores or nominate a giving tree to defray honeymoon costs. Sites such as honeyfund.com make it easy for guests to contribute toward honeymoon airfares, accommodations, and day-trips.

GIVING TREES

Many couples today live together before marriage and already have a well-stocked home. In that case, a modest check might be welcome instead of a household gift, for the couple to spend as they wish. This suggestion requires tact and discretion; once again, mention of it does not belong in the wedding invitation. It should be sent by someone else, perhaps the mothers of the couple rather than the bridal couple. For example:

A little word from Miriam and Jan regarding Artiom and Melissa's nuptials. We have received inquiries as to where they are registered. In fact, they have chosen not to have a registry, as they have been sharing a home these past few years. If you wish, a modest check would be gratefully received. That said, please know that this is a suggestion only.

AVOID "PRESENTATIONS ONLY"...

Some couples have a sneaky way of dodging unwanted wedding gifts. By putting "presentations only" on their invitations, they're essentially demanding that guests present checks or cash only. I beg you to avoid this practice.

...AND "ENDOWING A CHAIR"

I was mystified when I first heard about "endowing a chair" years ago. I thought it had something to do with a professorial chair at a college faculty; in fact, it was a bold-faced request for a monetary amount equal to the cost of the guest's meal! I was staggered and almost burst into flames on the spot. Unless your marriage is a public event, this has no place. I raise this issue not because I think you would actually do it, but because it's worth knowing about. It bears repeating: a wedding gift in no way needs to reflect the cost of your hospitality.

Please don't confuse this with the Italian tradition of willingly choosing a gift that covers the cost of the meal; it's all a question of intent. In this example, guests are not being prevailed upon to meet a financial minimum; they are choosing to bestow a gift of equal or more perceived value.

...BUT DO EMBRACE THE CHARITY OPTION

Charitable donations can be a very gracious alternative or inclusion to the traditional gift registry. Friends of ours offered guests the option to donate to the couple's favorite charity, a foundation supporting Tourette's syndrome, in lieu of a gift. Including a cause dear to their hearts is a lovely thing for a couple to do; it acknowledges the abundance in their own life while helping someone else.

THANK-YOU CARDS

A Savvy Bride takes the time to thank each guest *in writing* for his or her gift. Yes, even in this digital age. Do not send a group email (perish the thought!) or even an individual email, unless your guest lives on the North Pole or the International Space Station. I blanch when I see a group note on the tables at weddings, saying "Please accept our thanks for your good wishes and gifts." Sorry: *no*. People deserve more than that, as they have spent time, money, and effort indulging you with all manner of creature comforts as you begin married life. Show them your style with a graciously penned note. Traditionally, you have one year to send it, but I'd aim to have it done by the three-month mark.

And a little grace goes a long way when a guest appears to be wading in different financial waters currently than at previous family celebrations:

A few years ago, I attended a family wedding and gifted a rather expensive objet d'art to a niece and her husband. Then I had a career change and went back to grad school—so there was much less money to bestow an opulent gift. At the next wedding, I could afford only a modest kitchen gadget. The bride-to-be and her mother were fabulous and gracious. "You gave the very best you could each time. How could we be anything but appreciative?" the bride said. It struck me as very graceful. —MORGAN, SYDNEY

⟁ *Global Glimpses*

The standard wedding gift for a **Japanese** couple is cash, called *oshugi*, often handed out in decorative envelopes, *shugi-bukuro*.

Guests to **Muslim** weddings often present the bride and groom with eggs, as these gifts symbolize fertility.

Guests to **Irish** weddings often bestow bells as a wedding gift for the couple's new home. When a disagreement bubbles, one of them is supposed to ring the bell to end the argument peacefully.

PART VII

Though It's Rare . . .

Chapter Eighteen

IT HAPPENS: LET'S CALL
THE WHOLE THING OFF

⋙⋘

IT MIGHT BE UNCOMMON, BUT I'd be remiss not to address the issue of a wedding being called off, because this is a time when a lady's sense of grace really needs to come into its own.

The reasons for a cancellation are as varied and numerous as the couples themselves. But one common factor does enter into play when considering how and when to break the news: how soon before the nuptials the decision was made.

If we're talking months before the wedding day, the parents can issue a brief note, thank people for their good wishes at this difficult time, and let them know that any gifts will be returned.

If the decision comes far later, mere weeks before the wedding, friends and family can be recruited to discreetly spread the word as soon as possible. A trusted friend or relative can be dispatched to promptly contact guests who would be traveling any distance to attend.

If the time frame is days or hours before, someone needs to be appointed to each venue in case anyone misses the memo.

Sometimes it's simply too late to cancel a reception, and here, a little creativity can provide a gracious and generous solution. One Savvy Bride contacted a nearby retirement community to donate a beautiful dinner; another had the caterer pack up the meal and deliver it to a homeless shelter.

All that's needed is dignity, the briefest of explanations (if any), and a willingness to graciously move on.

EPILOGUE

You've done it!

You've negotiated, soothed nerves, and navigated dozens of decisions with aplomb. Step back and take a breath. You've earned it. Survey your handiwork: you've created a joyous and stylish celebration!

When you're ready, see *The Savvy Bride's Guide: Your Wedding Checklist* in the lead-up to the final three-month countdown.

You will be a *stunning* bride. Enjoy your day and the new chapter that awaits.

My best to you and your partner,
Alicia
savvylife.net

ACKNOWLEDGMENTS

I've so enjoyed researching and writing this book. Along the way, I have once again benefited from much support and wisdom to shape its contents and flow. To these people I offer my heartfelt thanks:

Support Team
To Holly Young, to whom this book is dedicated, and whose natural sense of savvy is both an inspiration and, yes, a source of slight envy; to Charmaine Lobo (loboluxe.com and intrepidallergymum.com) for her treasured insight, savvy business acumen, and for posing just the right question at just the right time, when I wanted to give up and flee to Kazakhstan under an assumed name; to Christina Street (née Riviere) for her effortless grace, giving nature, and unwavering support across publishing issues and far beyond; to Megan Cammilleri (née Pegrum) for her artistic eye and for inspiring me with her patience, humor, and inner strength; to Ihaan Adriansz and Tania D'Ercole for their thoughtful and considered feedback, which both boosts me and challenges me to think through a different prism; to Astor and Lourdette Adriansz and Jo-Anne Morel, for their continued support, enduring friendship, and insight; to Michael Corbett and Jacinta Corbett for their unrelenting support; to Grace Mattioli (gracemattioli.com) for her trusted friendship and for so generously sharing her experience in the publishing world; to Grace Conti for her cultural insight, wisdom, and warmth.

And most of all to Jon, whose voice on a phone can both calm me down and perk me up in the same moment, and whose laughter is my shorthand for happiness. Your key in the door is one of my favorite sounds.

Editorial Team
To copyeditor Theresa Duran (duraneditorial.com) for her extraordinary depth of experience and a trained focus that could just as easily have been deployed in espionage; to Amy Apel (amyapel.com) for her industry, insight, and an index I am proud to show.

Design Team

To Anne Keenan Higgins (annekeenanhiggins.com), once again, for her stylish, delicious Savvy Bride cover art; to Lynn Bell of Monroe Street Studios (monroest.com) for her beautiful interior design, which balances whimsy with substance and for her creative input on the cover; to Lisa Fulton (48hrbooks.com) for her early-stage interior design and cover input on both editions of this book; to Elizabeth Shrier for her author photo and sense of fun (elizabethshrier.com).

Legal Counsel

To Alan Korn (alankorn.com) for his sound legal advice.

Further Thanks

Pingkan Smith (trimtummy.com.au), Rashmi Singhvi, Rohita Kandula, Julie Calliss, Rose Cruz Cuison Villazor, Roza Ibragimova, Zoe Deadman, Mary Elbakyan, Cynthia House Nooney (cynthianooney.com), Tirza Kramer, Kathy Laucius (thetimeisnowfitness.com), Daniela Loga, Kirby O'Connell (styleknockout.blogspot.com), Soledad Tanner, Jen Glantz (bridesmaidforhire.com), Jane Harley, Lucy Segal, Karen Willis Holmes (karenwillisholmes.com), Tiffany Merklinger, Matt Rabe, Amanda Roise (artofroise.com). And to the ladies who preferred only their first name be used: Brenda, Skylar, Stella, Kathy, Gemma, Harriett, Faith, Carolina, Jana, A.J., Mia, Miriam, Lupita, Marlene, Karla, Millie, Aubree, Morgan, and Mariska.

Acknowledgment of Trademarks and Copyright

The author thanks the following artists and companies, and acknowledges their rightful ownership of their corresponding trademarks and service marks: Matt Groening, creator of the series *The Simpsons* (Fox Broadcasting Company, 1989–) and its cartoon matriarch Marge Simpson, known for her towering blue hair; The Divine Miss M, Bette Midler; also eBay; Facebook; Pinterest; Skype; Twitter.

Disclosure and Disclaimer

In full journalistic disclosure, I advise that I appear in some anecdotes under a different name. Anonymity was more discreet. Also, some contributors chose a pseudonym or asked that I allocate one for privacy.

Further Reading

The list is kept fresh on my website at savvylife.net.

Book Club Discussion Sheets

Also on my website at savvylife.net.

SELECT BIBLIOGRAPHY

Chapter Three

Indian tycoon: "India: Gem Trader Funds 'Mass Fatherless Wedding,'" BBC News, December 1, 2014, http://www.bbc.com/news/blogs-news-from-elsewhere-30277379.

Chapter Five

Slaying a chicken: "Mongolian Marriage Customs," ChinaCulture.org, http://www.chinaculture.org/focus/focus/minzuwang/2007-08/14/content_383147.htm.

Statistical modeling for guest list: Tim Harford, "Guest List Angst—A Statistical Approach," *Financial Times*, October 11, 2013, http://www.ft.com/cms/s/2/a59e1070-307b-11e3-80a4-00144feab7de.html#axzz-3TYOpRwdM.

Chapter Nine

Mauritania fat farms: "The Fat Farms of Mauritania," Vice News, May 2013, http://www.vice.com/video/the-fat-farms-of-mauritania.

Chapter Ten

Moonie mass weddings: "Moonies Hold Mass Wedding in South Korea," *The Guardian*, March 3, 2015, http://www.theguardian.com/world/2015/mar/03/moonies-mass-wedding-south-korea-unification-church-hak-ja-han-sun-myung-moon.

ABOUT THE AUTHOR

Alicia Young is an Australian television journalist with more than fifteen years' experience in local, national, and international news. Her passion for current events propelled her to Russia (where she presented the news in Moscow), the US, UK, and Europe. She has contributed to newsrooms around the world as an anchor, medical reporter, and international correspondent. She has worked with Walter Cronkite, filed live reports from Rome on the death of Pope John Paul II, covered various presidential elections/inaugurations, and reported on the aftermath of the magnitude 8.8 earthquake that rocked Chile in 2010.

Alicia was once told off by Mother Teresa for not having children (she forgot) and has volunteered at a hospice and leprosy hospital in Kolkata, India. Outside work, Alicia handles parasols and power tools with equal ease (not really, but she helpfully holds the flashlight while her better half fixes things around the house).

Alicia is a dynamic and engaging speaker, drawing on her global travel and background in television and radio news to weave a story around a range of topics.

She is based in the US.

Learn more at savvylife.net.

A REQUEST

I hope you've enjoyed my book and perhaps gleaned an idea or two. If you have a moment, I would very much appreciate a quick Amazon review! You can find a link on my website, savvylife.net.

INDEX

friends
advice from, 13
announcing engagement to, 19
destination weddings and, 22
gracious behavior toward,
12–13, 25, 56
professional services of, 35–36,
91, 113
wedding dress shopping and,
66–67

G
garlic, 107
garter tossing, 89
German wedding traditions, 37,
93
gift bags, 93
gift registries, 119–120
gifts, 36, 119–122, 125
gift tables, 90
giving trees, 120
glass, smashing of, 85
glory boxes, 119
gowns, 65–73
gracious bridal behavior
being a savvy bride, 12
in canceling a wedding,
125–126
toward family members, 34,
40–41, 67
toward friends, 12–13, 25, 56
toward groom, 12, 33
toward on-site service providers,
111
responses to rude comments, 20
wedding gifts, 119–122
grandparents, 18, 59, 60, 109–
110, 112–113
graphic designers, 61–62

Greek wedding traditions, 26, 85,
93
grooms, 8, 12, 13–14, 19, 22–23,
33–34, 116
groomsmen, 28–29, 59, 87, 115
guest books, 25
guest lists, 34, 41, 45–47, 53–54
guests, 58–60, 91–92, 112

H
hair stylists, 74
haldi ceremonies (India), 75
headdresses, 69
health insurance, 44
heirlooms, 21, 67
henna designs, 75
Hindu weddings, 116
home receptions, 115–116
honeyfund.com, 120
honeymoons, 14, 88, 93, 120
hope chests, 119

I
Indian (India) wedding traditions,
37, 45, 75, 90, 99, 109, 116
insects, 106
interfaith ceremonies, 84
invitations, 45–47, 61–62
Irish wedding traditions, 45, 104,
107, 122
Italian wedding traditions, 45, 121
itemization of price quotes, 55

J
Japanese wedding traditions, 69,
75, 122
Jewish wedding traditions, 21, 62,
82, 83–84
jua-jui (ring games), 90